I0649858

ALSO BY T. BYRAM KARASU, M.D.

❧

*The Art of Serenity: The Path to a Joyful Life*
*in the Best and Worst of Times*

# THE SPIRIT OF HAPPINESS

DISCOVERING GOD'S PURPOSE

FOR YOUR LIFE

T. BYRAM KARASU, M.D.

SIMON & SCHUSTER

NEW YORK   LONDON   TORONTO   SYDNEY

SIMON & SCHUSTER
Rockefeller Center
1230 Avenue of the Americas
New York, NY 10020

For information about special discounts for bulk purchases,
please contact Simon & Schuster Special Sales:
1-800-456-6798 or business@simonandschuster.com.

Designed by Davina Mock

Manufactured in the United States of America

10  9  8  7  6  5  4  3  2  1

Library of Congress Cataloging-in-Publication Data is available.

ISBN-13: 978-0-7432-8903-0
ISBN-10:    0-7432-8903-X

# ACKNOWLEDGMENTS

*For I am thy passing guest, a sojourner, like all my fathers.*

Ps. 39:12 (RSV)

Not only the spiritual, but also the intellectual heritage of this book belongs to our biblical fathers. Each chapter incorporates messages and quotations distilled from the Bible, which serves as a philosophy of life. Many of my acknowledgments, therefore, must remain primarily with those immortal *sojourners*.

There were, of course, many exceptionally talented *passing guests* who contributed to the genesis of this book. Foremost, I am profoundly indebted to Sydny Miner, senior editor at Simon & Schuster, for her enthusiasm and dedication to this project. This is the second book on which she and I have collaborated. Sydny's unwavering critical review and uncommon literary skills enabled me to express my ideas with greater precision and clarity.

I am most thankful to Katie de Koster for her meticulous copyediting; to Sarah Hochman, for her gracious and competent responsiveness; to Davina Mock, for her elegant design; to Victoria Meyer and Aileen Boyle, for their heartfelt marketing endeavors on my behalf; to Loretta Denner, production editor, for pulling the book together with such masterly guidance.

ACKNOWLEDGMENTS

I am immensely grateful to Tina Marie Bonanno, for her exemplary judgment, hard work, and invaluable literary assistance; to Josephine Costa, for her extraordinary and adept organizational contributions; to Hilda Cuesta, for her divine presence and remarkable efficiency in the preparation of the manuscript; and to Angela Toscano, for her expertise in technical challenges.

I thank my wife, Sylvia Karasu, as well, for her sage advice and scholarly vision throughout this journey.

# CONTENTS

# INTRODUCTION

# THE BIBLE ON MY MIND:
## CHAPTER AND VERSE

*. . . eternal purpose . . . is filled with all fullness of God.*

Eph. 3:11, 19 (NIV)

I have practiced psychiatry for the last thirty-five years. I have written many articles and books about psychological care and sought out factors that might help people to be happy. I've studied the works of many psychologists and philosophers, and I have read the popular books that explore sources of happiness and the meaning of life. They deliver advice on self-actualization, success at work, relationships, marriage, world views, and philosophies of living. The proliferation of these "self-ultimacy" books validates my conviction that the answer to the human dilemma can't be found in the realm of the mind. The works of secular gurus demonstrate again and again that making the mind of man its own center generates only personal confusion, unhappiness, and communal disorders.

In my book *The Art of Serenity,* I identified six tenets of soulfulness and spirituality as the basic requirements for happiness: The Love of Others, The Love of Work, The

Love of Belonging, Believing in the Sacred, Believing in Unity, and Believing in Transformation. I emphasized that a secular person may cultivate these extraordinary tenets, but it will be difficult to maintain them without divine inspiration.

This book begins where *The Art of Serenity* ended, with the belief in and the love of God. This book will guide you to the next and final step: to become godly.

To believe—to have faith—in God means trusting that there is a reason for the existence of everything in this world and beyond, and that there is meaning in its mystery. It means believing that there is a Holy Purpose. To be godly means to resonate with God's Holy Purpose, to bring all your personal and mundane purposes under its umbrella. If you not only have faith, but also become godly, you'll be a recipient of God's help, friendship, and boundless generosity in every aspect of your life.

In this book I use the Bible as the only source of reference. Throughout the centuries, men of wisdom have praised the Bible's guidance for truthful living; its cheerful urgings of love and compassion; its eternal lessons of serenity amidst the tribulations and adversities of the world; its tender teachings of the mysteries of life. As Heinrich Heine says in *Ludwig Boerne* (1840), "Great and wide as the world, rooted in the abysmal depths of creation and rising aloft into the blue mysteries of heaven . . . sunrise and sunset, promise and fulfillment, birth and death, the whole human drama, everything is in this book. It is the Book of Books, *Biblia*."

I am not a man of the cloth, merely a student of the human dilemma. Any theologian who reads this book will easily see the hand of a layman at work and I hope will forgive any of my shortcomings. With that proviso, I will present how you can find God's Holy Purpose and become godly. I will describe what godliness means in all aspects of your life, ranging from your career to relationships with your spouse, children, friends, and colleagues, and even strangers.

Only by being godly can you be strong and successful, find joy and happiness, and live an extraordinarily meaningful existence while leading an ordinary life.

# THE
# SPIRIT OF
# HAPPINESS

*There is naught in the Gospels, which does not shine and illuminate the world by its splendor, so that even things that seem trifling and unimportant shine with the majesty of the Holy Spirit.*

St. Jerome, *The Commentary on Ezekiel,* c. A.D. 410–415

# CHAPTER I

# GOD'S HOLY PURPOSE

*Know where you are headed.*

Prov. 4:26 (CEV)

Identifying your purpose in life is the toughest task you'll ever face. But once you define your purpose, the meaning of your life will become clearer and all other tasks, no matter how difficult they may seem, will become easier.

You can't find the meaning of your life just by living. Life is like an enormous map. The map shows where you *could* go, but it won't tell you where you *should* go. The destination you should head to must come from within. The Bible says, *Know where you are headed and you will stay on solid ground.* (Prov. 4:26, CEV) Of course, the logical question is: "How will I know my destination?"

Before you can understand the travels you will make, you must understand the traveler—yourself. Then comes the next obvious question: "How do I understand myself?" The answer: by understanding God. The Bible says, *The only accurate way to understand ourselves is by what God is.* (Rom. 12:3, MSG) God informs you and He informs life.

The Holy Spirit will set you afire and you'll find your purpose by knowing the will of God.

Lack of purpose undermines you more than any handicap. You may know people who are blind, deaf, or wheelchair-bound but function in life undeterred. They teach, run companies, write books, play musical instruments. People excel—whether physically challenged or not—because they are greatly committed to what they are doing. Their enthusiasm for living encompasses the totality of their beings, including their relationships with friends, spouses, children, other members of the family, and communities. Their purpose becomes their mission and the source of the meaning in their lives. They have learned to *center their lives in God.* (2 Chron. 14:4, MSG)

Without meaning, life becomes too heavy a burden. Legend tells us that even Moses suffered from a loss of meaning. When he began walking down from Mount Sinai holding the two heavy stone tablets inscribed with the Ten Commandments, he carried them easily. But when Moses saw the Israelites worshipping the golden calf, God's words disappeared from the stone tablets and they became too heavy for Moses to carry. They were just blank stone slabs, and without the Ten Commandments, Moses lost his mission. He cried out in despair: *"Erase me out of the book you've written."* (Exod. 32:32, MSG) He had lost his purpose.

You may ask the most difficult question: "How do I understand God?" You cannot reach God by thinking, wondering, and reasoning. These are activities of your mind. God is beyond the realm of the mind. Understanding God and understanding how to reach God are products of faith. You find God by devout contemplation, not through your mind's reasoning. The mind makes inferences and imagines, but God is not inferable and imaginable. Because the mind is finite, it cannot contemplate the Infinite Being. But if you push your mind out of the way, you might find God's most innate essence. Be a holy asker; the answers will come.

For someone who is accustomed to thinking critically, the leap to believing in God is a difficult one. But faith is generated, not through comprehension—a tool of the mind—but by simple devotional belief. You do not need tools. You do not need education. In our society the learned have always been praised, and rightly so. But the learned are at a disadvantage when it comes to spiritual enlightenment, because their minds interfere with the formation of sacred unknowing. Even theology falls short because it, too, involves the mind in talking about God, introducing the constraint of language, which can't really describe God. Enlightenment transcends all learning. Spiritual knowledge—holy wisdom—is obtained by seeking dissolution in God.

## TO KNOW THE HOLY PURPOSE IS TO DISSOLVE IN GOD

*Those who live in God's love live in God, and God lives in them.*

1 John 4:16 (GWT)

A very successful man, whose sentences frequently began with the word "I," joked that "God might hear me, but I cannot hear God." That is because God is audible only when "I" is silent. If you don't hear God, it is because you are exerting a will *not* to turn your ear toward God. Turn to Him the way a sunflower turns to the sun. You are God's flower on earth. Do you want to hear God? Stop saying "I." Say

"You." Don't be self-referential. Focus on God. God will hear you and you'll hear God.

A young scientist who fed all his life on the dry husks of facts and was determined to put me in my place asked: "How do you understand God?" I replied with my usual, "You don't get there by your mind; you have to make a quantum leap of faith." Seeing the dissatisfaction in his eyes, I tried a response that would resonate with his field of expertise: "My mind does not even understand a bee, let alone God." He kept quizzing me: "Has God ever spoken to you?" I guess he was wondering if I had ever had any auditory hallucinations. I said, "God speaks not only to me, but to all of us, to things and beings around us." He was relentless. "Have you ever seen God?" I said, "God is coexistent with us. We infer His existence from the existence of the universe."

Now the young scientist was as frustrated with me as I was with him. He asked, "Well, what is God exactly?" *"Exactly?* God is personified incomprehensibility. God is the ground of existence. He surrounds everything, encloses all, and is enclosed by none. He is the fountainhead of life, to be apprehended, not comprehended." The scientist snickered. "Those are just words. Do you honestly believe in miracles, like Jesus walking on water?" I replied, "The fact that we walk on earth is a miracle, never mind Jesus' walking on water."

It was my turn. I asked if he believed in the existence of creatures. He nodded. "Well then, why don't you believe in the Creator?" He smiled mischievously. "But where is the Creator?" And he quoted Job: *"If I go east, he isn't there. If I go west, I can't find him. If I go northward, . . . I can't observe him. If I turn southward, I can't see him."* (Job 23:8–9, GWT) I countered, *God, . . . I look behind me and you're there, then up ahead and you're there, too.* (Ps. 139:1, 5, MSG) God asks us: *"Am I not everywhere in all the heavens and earth?"* (Jer. 23:24, NLT)

Our five sensory organs are equipped to receive only their corresponding senses. The eye can see but cannot hear. Likewise, the mind can understand but cannot believe. The Bible says, *We don't look for things that can be seen but for things that can't be seen. Things that can be seen are only temporary. But things that can't be seen last forever.* (2 Cor. 4:18, GWT)

"Can you see love?" I asked the young scientist. "No," he replied. "Well, *'God is love,'* says the Bible." (1 John 4:8, GWT)

We assign God the best human (powerful, beautiful) and natural (infinite light to darkness) attributes, but God is beyond attributions. You will not find God as an object to be thought about, understood, or experienced. But you may find God in the laughter of your children; the grief of a friend; the opening of forsythias after a long winter; a covering of snow; the noisy joyfulness of birds and wind; or the quiet testimony of ants and cobwebs. God just is. God's altar is everywhere and in everything. Engage God through immersing yourself in His creations; you'll find that God is self-evident.

We live in a universe where you are both an insignificant particle at the mercy of the unknown and a significant person at the mercy of the unknowable. We perceive this situation as a threat to our existence, and yearn for certainty and control.

To control fate by attempting to know the universe or to know your psyche provides neither security nor freedom from anxiety. If anything, presumption of control generates insecurity and anxiety because life is not cut off from natural and spiritual orders. The only security is mooring in God; only God can anchor you from outside and within.

As you dissolve into God, you'll realize that the Creator and creation are one. There is no separate "I." In God your boundaries no longer exist. Your boundaries—physical body, mind, the things you own, job—are temporary phenomena, meant to serve your present transient existence. You are defined eternally only in communion with God, where there are no distinct beings and where all are one. This boundless communion and unity extends to all other creations of God as well—animals, vegetation, earth, skies, sunlight, morning mist, ocean waves, winds, and silence.

You don't need a reason other than witnessing your own existence in this immense universe to know that you should will what God wills. You are your own witness. Even in your most desperate moment, place your will in unison with God's will.

## DISSOLUTION IN GOD IS BOUNDLESS COMMUNION

*Spirit can be known only by spirit—God's Spirit*
*and our spirits in open communion.*

1 Cor. 2:14 (MSG)

Dissolution in God brings a blissful state of mind. It is the powerful calmness that you experienced, but can only emotionally remember, in your mother's womb: the imprinted sense of security; the complete trust that all will be taken care of; being fed and kept warm and protected; oneness with the mother. Dissolving yourself into the Divine Womb of God is such a security, a gentle unfolding into wholeness.

Seeking such comfort somewhere else or with someone else only turns you into a living example of longing. The only place where yearning can be fulfilled is in the sanctuary of God. There, God is, and all is fine.

In this primordial dissolution, you'll experience a trusting innocence and have a vague sense that you've been there before. You won't be mistaken. At the moment of your spiritual enlightenment, you will receive the second touch of God; the first one occurred at your conception. You have the potential for spiritual enlightenment because you are already seeded for it. You just have to bring yourself to the Divine Well.

You can get lost in an aimless or wrongly aimed lifetime if you stray too far from the Divine Well. Then, unless you know that you are lost, you'll never be found. But the closer you stay to God, the stronger you become. Think of your link to God in terms of a portable telephone handset at home. The farther you go from the base, the weaker the sound. When you replace the handset into the base, the phone recharges and no longer operates on battery but on a powerful, steady electrical current. Likewise, your proximity to the spirit empowers you with Divine Energy.

The path to dissolving in God is well identified but unpaved. Don't be discouraged by the process. Bringing your soul to the spirit may seem a slow, arduous journey but think of the joy of going home after a long, secular exile.

You have every reason to be optimistic about becoming enlightened. Given the miracle of your being, which came from not-being, the journey to becoming shouldn't be too difficult. Because God is imprinted on you at birth, everyone can rekindle the Holy Spirit within.

Eventually, your epiphany will come. It will be either in a

revelation, in which you'll be spiritually enlightened during a quantum leap of faith, as if God has touched you, or (more commonly) it will come through a slow, organic process of building faithfulness by the steady cultivation of your godly qualities—wooing God by following His footsteps. Once there is no space between you and God, you will be hit by enlightenment. You will find that you sense God and He breathes in you. You'll be gripped by the meaning of your existence.

- Existence is seamless and eternal.
- There are no separate entities or beings and things.
- Time is continuous: there is no past, present, or future.
- Space is ceaseless: there is no here, there, or else-where.

You still may be interested in visiting wonderful places, you may yearn for beautiful things and people, but once you find the supremacy of God—the distilled essence of love— the ardor for all other longing ends. You will find serenity, not by adding more things to your life, but by subtracting your desire for them.

As you cultivate God's values and venerate the Divine, you'll achieve a state of not desiring objects. Faith is the ulti-mate wealth.

Once you're delivered from the world of mind-made concepts, you're also emancipated from the confinements of time and place. Time and space are concepts, not distinct entities. There is no such thing as the year 2006 or 11 A.M. or Westport or New York. These are man-made concepts that help us negotiate the material world. In fact, time and space are neither linear nor circular. They are images of eternity.

People who are future-focused tend to be prone to anxiety. Regardless of whether the anticipated event is a pleasant one, such as a wedding, or an unpleasant one, such as a biopsy, it generates anxiety. You don't need to worry about the future or obsess and recycle your anticipatory thoughts again and again. When you are in communion with God, the future will be taken care of. ". . . *don't ever worry about tomorrow,"* the Bible says. (Matt. 6:34, GWT)

On the other hand, people who are past-focused tend to be prone to depression. You don't need to ruminate about the past, dwell obsessively upon or recycle your regrets, punish yourself for things you have done or failed to do, or perpetuate a litany of anger and resentment toward people in your past. The Bible says, *"Don't look back."* (Gen. 19:17, MSG)

Your greatest burden is feeling alone in anticipation of the future or in coming to terms with the past. As long as there is a space between you and God, you are alone. You can bear any pain, any deprivation, any suffering, if you don't have to bear it alone. When you achieve communion with God, you won't experience the past and future as separate from the present. In communion with God, all entities lose their separateness; the invisible is incarnate in the visible. In this mystical union, all locations cease to exist; the space between you and everything else disappears. Existence becomes a seamless continuity. In this divine dissolution, your anxieties and worries end. You feel an amazing sense of lightness, as if an enormous burden has been lifted from your shoulders. In fact, it has been.

## TO DISSOLVE IN GOD, BREATHE IN THE HOLY SPIRIT

*He breathed on them and said . . . , "Receive the Holy Spirit."*

John 20:22 (NLT)

As your lungs need pure air, your soul needs pure spirit. As your lungs need protection from air pollution, your soul needs protection from external pollution. For you to remain in good health, it is important that your lungs receive fresh air, not just be spared polluted air. Equally, your soul, besides being spared of inner and external pollution, must also breathe in the Holy Spirit to remain in good health.

The soul cannot be idle. The soul without the Holy Spirit can go in any direction: it can love but be unfaithful; it can work but be misdirected; it can belong, but wrongly. Dissolving in God anchors your soul. The unanchored soul seeks harbor elsewhere: in money, sex, drugs, alcohol, fame, and power. God is the only safe harbor. The Holy Spirit guides your soul, at times energizes it, at times contains it, but always shows it the path to salvation.

Constantly remind yourself to breathe in the Holy Spirit, even after it becomes as natural and spontaneous as breathing air. This breathing in may initially take the form of worship and prayer. Later, it may occur in simple contemplation, such as sitting in a quiet sanctuary or humming a hymn.

## BREATHE IN THE HOLY SPIRIT THROUGH WORSHIP

*That's the kind of people the Father is . . . looking for: those who are simply and honestly themselves before him in their worship.*

John 4:23 (MSG)

Worship is joyful submission and faithful surrender, not an organized atrophy or a social sedation; it taps our deepest spiritual energies. Joyful submission is not a "will to perish." It is witnessing eternal infinity. Faithful surrender is not a religious act, a doctrinal compliance, a defeat of autonomy, an acceptance of weakness, or a declaration of helplessness. It is faithful harboring in God and trusting His love and benevolence.

Faithful surrender is neither self-mortification nor resignation to external events. Surrender infuses you with the power of God and gives you the spiritual energy to find ways out of or through difficult life circumstances. It is inner docility to God's will.

- Still your mind.
- Seek tender composure.
- Struggle.
- Surrender.

Worship is not a time- and place-specific activity; it need not involve attending services, following rituals, or participating in religious ceremonies and duties. Worshipping God is a way of being—all the time and everywhere. Worship is carried out in all activities, whether you are driving a bus, cleaning dishes, playing with your children, making love to your spouse, or doing nothing. In fact, your every heartbeat should remind you of God's presence. In return, you resonate with God's spirit with every breath that you take. The Bible says, *The kingdom of God is within you.* (Luke 17:21, NLT)

The religious person believes in God; the worshipper loves God. Being religious is being obedient and faithful. Being a worshipper of "the known God" is joyful. God remains unknown to him or her who believes in God but does not love Him. The Bible says, *So love the Lord your God with all your heart, with all your soul, with all your mind, and with all your strength.* (Mark 12:30, GWT)

When you believe in and love God, you offer and surrender yourself to Him to be freed from your personal bondage. But selfless offering and loving surrender aren't forms of giving up your responsibilities. If anything, they expand your commitments. They are the acceptance of the Divine Order. Worship brings peaceful coexistence with your friends, coworkers, and family members. Worship stops you from playing God and allows you to accept God's will. You won't need to pull and push other people or maneuver or manipulate circumstances. Consequently you won't be disliked, feared, defended against or fought with; rather you'll be liked and assisted in your goals. In communion with God and in loving His other fellows, there is no need for polarization in relationships, such as being in control versus being controlled; dominating versus being dominated. Worship brings you freedom from these depleting conflicts and enables you to preserve your energy to serve your mission better.

## BREATHE IN THE HOLY SPIRIT THROUGH PRAYING

*Never stop praying.*

1 Thess. 5:17 (GWT)

"I wish I had time for prayer; I just don't have any. I am so busy," said a man who seemed to me to have a thin soul. I suggested that he find some time to be with God by cutting down on the time he spent with others, including me.

Prayer is a means to one goal: being with God. Don't pray to be rich, or successful, to own things or to achieve worldly accomplishments. God doesn't tune in to these frequencies. People who remain in a childhood relationship with their parents, one in which they express wishes and demand they be granted, may replicate that pattern with God. God has higher expectations from His adult children. God does not hear self-serving pleas and if He does His inevitable answer is, as Matthew urged, *Grow up.* (Matt. 5:48, MSG)

Praying about your health may be self-serving. For example, should you ask God to cure your cancer or heart ailment? Should you pray to God to end the suffering of a friend or for peace on earth? These seem to be selfless and innocent prayers. Actually these prayers assume that God isn't aware of or doesn't care about suffering or world conflicts, and that He needs your prayers to be prompted or persuaded to do a good deed. But God knows everything, cares about everything, and does exactly what must be done. You don't know God's reason for perpetuating conflicts around the world or for not alleviating a person's suffering. To pray that God should stop these events is grandiose and presumptuous.

You may rightly ask, "How then do I pray? If I cannot pray for self-interested, mundane, or altruistic purposes, then what do I pray for?" It is difficult to answer these questions if you associate prayer with requests. But it is easier to answer if you think of prayer as contemplation. You can meditate on godly values. For example, you may ask, "How can I be more a loving and compassionate person?" or you can just still your mind and let the answer blossom in the silence.

Praying is primarily a calm and disciplined silence. It is

God's language and the language of all tongues and creatures, a silent and effortless communion. Praying is also an
interactive covenant between you and God. In your youth
you may wish for things to be—representing your youthful
hopes. In your adulthood you may wish to have the wisdom
to accept things as they are—representing your yearnings
for maturity. In your mature years you may wish nothing—
representing your cultivation of gratitude. That is the Holy
Contemplation.

Prayer is the language of the soul that seeks the Holy
Spirit. Prayer is intended to bring a stillness of mind and a
tender composure of body. In contemplating God, you need
to stop all discursive thinking and all distracting moods and
bring your mind to a total standstill. This will pave the path
to reflective presence with God. In prayer you express your
longing to encounter God without seeking God's favor or
invoking God for selfish demands. In prayer God meets you
from within. There, you contemplate how to achieve something—not wish that it be granted. Prayers can be as
straightforward and innocent as "How may I live more
gracefully?" and "What should I do to be saved?"

In Holy Contemplation your soul asserts only its submission. Praying in its purest form is a meditation on God. You
withdraw your heart from all earthly thoughts to commune
and be alone with God. Prayer is putting yourself into a devotional frame of mind to seek (but not to try to change)
God's will. Prayer helps you obey His will and make it your
own. The purest, most pious prayer is the one that asks for
nothing. The best prayer is an expression of gratefulness, independent of life circumstances, even in an earthly Hell. A
woman who had an inoperable cancer made her daily
prayers confirm the sacredness of her illness: "Thank you,

God, for everything, including my cancer; I have no complaint whatsoever and I have no request of any sort."

Pray with all your faculties, not only with words and the silences, but by your behavior and your very being. Worshipping God isn't an activity isolated from the rest of your life. Words are abstract contemplations; action is the concrete manifestation of your faith. The outer company you keep is a place of social holiness—a place to reenact your prayers. If you want to speak with God, you first have to speak with people; if you want to work for God, you first have to work with people.

Prayer without faith has no wings. A man whose specific, self-serving prayers went unanswered said contemptuously that he would never again "believe in this faith business." He claimed he was too smart to fall for such unreasonable fables. As in the story of the pickpocket who meets a saint and sees only the saint's pocket, this man saw only God's pockets. He tried to argue that intellect was the reason for his lack of faith. But faith is ascension beyond reason; it is a deferential incredulity. If none of the man's prayers were answered, it was because he possessed only the form of prayer, not its essence. Only faith gives power to the prayer. Even then, God may respond to the faithful's prayer on His own terms. God may not come to the hungry in the form of food or to the thirsty in the form of water or to the sick in the form of a cure. The prayer that presupposes faith and trust in God breathes hope into expectations.

If your present life is empty of any holy purpose and even if you are far from deserving of being saved, pray to redeem yourself by seeking faith. God will pour Himself into your emptiness when you are ready.

## ALL OR NONE: THE NATURE OF FAITH

*God never abandons us.*

2 Cor. 4:9 (NLT)

Sometimes you may be impatient with God; for example, you may feel He is too slow to respond. The Bible says, *The Lord is not slow in keeping his promise, as some understand slowness.* (2 Pet. 3:9, NIV) Occasionally you may find yourself doubting God or quarreling or wrestling with God. God still welcomes you. But you must never abandon Him. When in doubt, repeat again and again, as God has said to us, *"I will not dishonor my promise or alter my own agreement."* (Ps. 89:34, GWT)

Meditating about God and loving and obeying God are activities of faithful submission. But not all of us get there without doubting, questioning, testing, and even quarreling, much the way that Job proceeded: *"So I won't keep my mouth shut, but I will speak from the distress that is in my spirit and complain about the bitterness in my soul."* (Job 7:11, GWT) Wrestling with God may be noisy and disturbing and that, too, is wonderful. You get to God either way. You may be crystal clear in your belief in God and passionately, deeply, and intimately know him. Or you may be equally clear in your belief in God's absence and passionately negate Him. Either way, your passionate engagement with God will bring you close to Him.

God reassures you. The true believer obviously doesn't question the validity of this statement. It may seem a little strange to assert that negating God may bring you close to Him, but that is how God works. Push Him away; He will pull you in. The more passionate your negation, the more powerfully you'll be pulled in. Just let it happen.

Believing in God isn't only a spiritual or religious matter. It is all encompassing. If you don't believe in God, it is quite likely that you don't believe in humanity either: most likely you doubt the loyalty of your spouse, the honesty of your partner, the genuineness of your friends.

The path to God is through a small, narrow gate. It demands sacrifice, resilience, and determination. *Enter through the narrow gate because the gate and road that lead to destruction are wide. Many enter through the wide gate. But the narrow gate and the road that lead to life are full of trouble. Only a few people find the narrow gate.* (Matt. 7:13-14, GWT) You cannot be a part-time, "quantified" believer. Some people become believers when they are in trouble. They or a loved one may be ill; they may have suffered certain losses and tragedies. Such "rainy-day believing" tends to be inauthentic, especially if the person reverts to indifference after the crises is resolved.

You cannot be a "qualified" believer either. Some people qualify God's scope: "I believe in the Creator but not in eternity." "I believe in compassion, but not for everyone." Such conditional belief is not belief in God. You need to believe in God totally, all the time, everywhere, and in every circumstance. The Spirit gives nothing to you until you give everything to Him. God says, *"When you look for me, you will find me. When you wholeheartedly seek me, I will let you find me,"* (Jer. 29:13, GWT) Then you will be offered the purpose of your life—*your* Holy Purpose.

# EXERCISES FOR PSYCHO-SPIRITUAL FITNESS

## THE WISDOM LEARNED FROM THE BIBLE

*God wants me to know my purpose.*

## MEDITATIVE EXERCISE OF SELF-REVELATION

*Have I understood myself enough
to know my purpose?*

## PRAYER EXERCISE OF GRATITUDE

*Dear God, thank You for knowing me.*

## INTENTIONAL EXERCISE OF SPIRITUAL REALIGNMENT

*I'll have faith and know God's will.*

*I wish to show that there is one wisdom which is perfect, and that this is contained in the Scriptures.*

Roger Bacon, *Opus Majus,* 1267

# CHAPTER II

# MAN'S HOLY PURPOSE
# IS STRIVING TO BE GODLY

*You were . . . created to be like*
*God, truly righteous and holy.*

Eph. 4:24 (GWT)

Man's Holy Purpose is to strive to be a godlike being: loving, caring, compassionate, peaceful.

God set the stage for you to inherit His goodness when He declared, *"Let us make humans in our image, in our like-ness."* (Gen. 1:26 GWT) You're born carrying an empty pot that is filled quickly with your inheritance from God—His values. In fact, *God lives in us.* (1 John 4:12, GWT) All you need is to be content with your inheritance. The Bible says, *A godly life brings huge profits to people who are content with what they have.* (1 Tim. 6:6, GWT)

Your existence with God is based on a covenant to be part of God's purpose, and do His work on Earth. All you need is faith to know what that work entails. *Anyone who has faith in me will do what I have been doing.* (John 14:12, NIV)

In Proverbs we are told, *The LORD . . . offers his friend-ship to the godly.* (Prov. 3:32, NLT) God will help you gain

His purpose if you accept His friendship. That friendship requires you to be grounded in the love and law of God and to be encompassed in the Divine Nature of God.

God's Divine Love demands that you nurture love, compassion, trustworthiness, and dependability in all your relationships and circumstances. His Divine Law demands that you refrain from pursuing unholy purposes.

When external forces, such as religion, impose Divine Love and Divine Law, these set the stage for a common human dilemma: resist or comply. You can secure genuine love and embrace its laws only by internalizing the Divine. When you experience the Divinity internally, spiritual enlightenment comes effortlessly. You won't have to decide to resist or comply because there are no external rules, only inner communion. If you don't stand apart from God, you are within God, and dwelling within the Divine is a way of being godlike.

Try to be godly but don't try to be God. If anything, be unassuming. The Bible says: *When you do good deeds, don't try to show off.* (Matt. 6:1, CEV) Being godly is the opposite of wanting to be comparable to God. Omnipotence and omniscience are irreducible powers. Pretending to possess them brings the delusional attitudes assumed by some people who are very successful in their work, profession, or business. These people esteem their mind as their God. Pursuing excessive wealth, power, and success are unholy ambitions that tend to generate insecure grandiosity. Those who pursue the unholy purpose—no matter how strong they might be—will find no peace.

Pursuing a Holy Purpose brings you a peaceful existence in the midst of human drama. The attitude of the godly person is humble but secure, serious but genial, self-confident but modest. Godly people are never afraid of doubt, but are always reassured. To them all power and omniscience belong only to God. Your highest possible virtue is to know the goodness God has created and to emulate His love, compassion, and holiness.

Of course, no one leads an entirely virtuous life. If you intend to remain virtuous, you may merit and receive God's promise of a bright and beautiful life and, more important, you may become more like Him. The Bible says you'll then witness *our lives gradually becoming brighter and more beautiful as God enters our lives and we become like him.* (2 Cor. 3:18, MSG)

A single virtuous act doesn't make you virtuous. Being godly changes the way you relate to others in your life and the way you connect to the material world. It alters your disposition toward other races, creeds, and nations. Godliness isn't directed at any one thing, but at everyone and everything. Once you reach a godly state, you automatically become faithful, whether you are working, having sex, parenting, or relating to members of your community.

## ORDINARY GODLINESS IS HOLY

*"Be holy."*

Lev. 19:2 (GWT)

Being godly does not mean living an extraordinary life; if anything, godly people live ordinary lives. As an enlightened person you'll have a loving family and friends, and you'll knit yourself into your community. But your faith will create extraordinary, daily small miracles for you, and you'll experience firsthand the power of the Holy Purpose.

> *A person with a holy purpose is*
> - enlightened
> - content and grateful
> - compassionate
> - humble
> - generous
> - peaceful and serene

Being godly does not mean you must engage in extraordinary acts, such as paying for a poor child's education or donating a kidney to a dying stranger. These are heroic gestures. But it is important to act in good faith in all your interactions and to be respectful of all people regardless of their station in life.

Godliness doesn't mean you need to drown out every earthly voice or that you need to become an ascetic disengaged from and resigned to the world. Godliness doesn't take the stance of the observer; it's not a form of inactivity. It doesn't mean giving up life or submitting to isolating impoverishment. Quite the contrary: you must be fully engaged in the world, be an active participant, and live comfortably. But while you live an ordinary life, you must be a receptive vessel for the mysteries of God.

Godliness isn't a task to be accomplished. It's a way of being, a mysterious illumination, a sort of holy ignorance. It doesn't have a specific end point. The spirituality of the godly is not supernatural power but divine vulnerability. Spiritual enlightenment is simplicity and naturalness; it doesn't mean you must be a person of extraordinary wisdom. It is being a person of ordinary common sense, possessing the wisdom of ordinariness. Ultimately, spirituality is a measure of your humanity—the ordinary holiness that God expects you to strive for: *Be holy because I, the LORD your God, am holy.* (Lev. 19:2, GWT)

# EXERCISES FOR PSYCHO-SPIRITUAL FITNESS

### THE WISDOM LEARNED FROM THE BIBLE

*God wants me to be like Him.*

### MEDITATIVE EXERCISE OF SELF-REVELATION

*Have I been a caring and compassionate being?*

### PRAYER EXERCISE OF GRATITUDE

*Dear God, thank You*
*for being who You are.*

### INTENTIONAL EXERCISE OF SPIRITUAL REALIGNMENT

*I will strive to be a godly person.*

## LOVE OF GOD WILL FUEL YOUR PURPOSE

*Pursue love, and desire spiritual gifts.*

1 Cor. 14:1 (GWT)

To pursue your Holy Purpose, you must have a place from which to start: the anchoring love of God.

> *Love is patient. Love is kind. Love isn't jealous. It doesn't sing its own praises. It isn't arrogant. It isn't rude. It doesn't think about itself. It isn't irritable. It doesn't keep track of wrongs. It isn't happy when injustice is done, but it is happy with the truth. Love never stops being patient, never stops believing, never stops hoping, never gives up. Love doesn't come to an end.*
>
> 1 Cor. 13:4-8 (GWT)

God's love isn't an abstract idea; it is a way of life. It's the undifferentiated base of love from which all other love flows. The Bible says, *Love means living the way God commanded us to live.* (2 John 1:6, NCV)

There is a great difference between healthy self-compassion—self-love—and unhealthy self-centeredness—unprincipled self-preoccupation. You first experience and acquire healthy self-love in the loving, approving gaze of your godly mother. It is a benign state of mind, a self-confidence that eventually is crystallized by your own love of God. Love you extend to God comes back as healthy self-love and seeds you with godlike qualities. Such love is transferable to your children, other intimates, and other people, including strangers. It promotes God's wish: *We were commanded to live in love.* (2 John 1:6, GWT)

Healthy self-love engenders a sense of communion with people, animals, and all of nature, even inanimate things. Healthy self-love is sharing the love of God. Sometimes healthy self-love doesn't come naturally. For example, you may not have received "I love you" and "You are lovable" messages from your parents. You may have to acquire the sense of being lovable by loving others. Although second-best to parental love, being lovable by loving others, when achieved, has the same spiritual effects on your relationships with others. Insecurities remaining in this cultivated self-love make you even more endearing.

God wants you to imitate Him. The Bible says so: *Imitate God.* (Eph. 5:1, GWT) This means that you love all of God's children and creatures. You extend a hand to those who are drowning in life, lift the paralyzed, see for the blind, hear for the deaf, and hug those who cannot touch. All encounters with your fellow beings should be filled with faith, hope, and love. The Bible says: *These three things will remain for ever. They are faith, hope, and love.* (1 Cor. 13:13, WE-NT) There is no such a thing as an insignificant relationship. Some people have a dismissive, if not contemptuous, predisposition. They think they are reserving their loving attitude for their intimates. Good faith is an all-or-nothing state of your soul. Only by loving all, respecting all, and trusting all can you love, respect, and trust one.

Being godly means aiming above all other psychological and philosophical concepts of humanity. It targets "goodness" in the sense of God's goodness—the ideal by which we live. For the godly person, everything has a moral dimension. Morality is the last word, not because you fear God, but because you share His love. You may fear God, but you cease being afraid of Him when His love takes up residence in your heart and removes all fears. The Bible says, *No fear exists where his love is. Rather, perfect love gets rid of fear.* (1 John 4:18, GWT)

Spiritual love is like a ladder. God is at the highest rung. From there, you step downward to share love with all other beings and things. Such encompassing love brings success and gives meaning to your every activity. The Bible says, *All things work together for good to them that love God, to them who are the called according to his purpose.* (Rom. 8:28, KJV) The love of God is the source of zestful and faithful engagement of the soul. It permanently centers you down deep to the core of spiritual existence. The Bible reasserts that *what matters is a faith that expresses itself through love.* (Gal. 5:6, GWT) It is this love that fuels all your Holy Purposes.

# EXERCISES FOR PSYCHO-SPIRITUAL FITNESS

## THE WISDOM LEARNED FROM THE BIBLE

*God wants love to be my greatest aim.*

## MEDITATIVE EXERCISE OF SELF-REVELATION

*Have I been living a life of love?*

## PRAYER EXERCISE OF GRATITUDE

*Dear God, thank You for loving me.*

## INTENTIONAL EXERCISE OF SPIRITUAL REALIGNMENT

*I'll be a love-bearer.*

## TRUST IN GOD DIRECTS YOUR PURPOSE

*With [God] is wisdom.*

Job 12:13 (ASV)

There is a story of a European town that was invaded by a band of marauders. The bandits rounded up all the towns-folk, herded them into the church, doused the building with gasoline, and set it ablaze. Several days later, a man from the town returned from a business trip to find the carnage. He picked through the ashes and thought he found the charred body of his ten-year-old daughter. With sorrow he buried her remains.

Seven years later, there was a knock at the door of the man's home, and the sound of a young woman's voice star-tled him from his mournful ruminations. The young woman called out, "Dad, it's your daughter. I wasn't killed in the fire. The bandits abducted me. I finally managed to escape them." The man refused to open the door, yelling for the girl to stop her cruel hoax and go away to leave him in his misery. The girl tried persuading him, first shouting and then sweetly pleading. Nothing worked. Finally she gave up and left, thinking her father was too ashamed to have her back.

Both father and daughter relied on their minds. Both came up with wrong answers.

There is no school for gaining wisdom and holy enlight-enment. Enlightenment is a form of knowledge that can't be learned; it can only be known by remembering that God is your source and that you must make God the center of your odyssey. Eternal wisdom doesn't require irrational senti-mentality or esoteric otherworldliness but deeply embracing a faithful life. What such a life reveals to you precedes the revelation of the Divine.

There is no wisdom independent of *light-bearers*—reflectors of the light of God. No philosophy provides you an alternative ideal or accomplishes a cohesive presentation of virtues. Only the Bible does. By a divine chemistry, faith is capable of transmuting even the most mundane activities in the world into meaningful and virtuous ones. The Bible offers Divine Guidance and gives meaning to our existence. It is the only sacredly optimistic and responsible stand that you need when taking a point of view for life. The Bible says: *"So then, be very careful how you live. Don't live like foolish people but like wise people."* (Eph. 5:15, GWT)

## GOD TEACHES YOU PROFOUND COMMON SENSE

*Every Scripture passage is inspired by God. All of them are useful for teaching, pointing out errors, correcting people, and training them for a life that has God's approval.*

2 Tim. 3:16 (GWT)

Magazines, books, and seminars by the hundreds try to teach you the basic knowledge of living. This so-called knowledge ranges from the complicated—how to raise children—to the banal—what and how much to eat. There are manuals offering advice on how to improve your sex life and how to exercise. You may listen to tapes about how to dress, relax, think, or even feel. In reality, all you need for living is common sense. The Bible says, *So I tell you to stop worrying about what you will eat or wear. Life is more than food, and the body is more than clothes.* (Luke 12:22–23, GWT)

Your recognition of visceral truth and profound common sense emanates from Divine Knowledge. Often, you don't use your common sense because you underestimate its value (especially when it comes to important matters), or your mind is so cluttered with information provided by experts that you can hardly see your internal light. Here's an example: You hear your baby crying in the middle of the night. Do you ignore the baby, as experts advise, so that she learns that crying won't bring an immediate response and so will learn to sleep uninterrupted in her crib? Or should you go to see what is going on? What does your visceral knowledge say to do? Pick up the baby, feed or rock or cuddle her, right? If your three-year-old sneaks into your bed, shivering with fear, do you entice, or worse, force him back to his own bed so that he becomes desensitized to fear? Or do you just let him occasionally come to your bed without making much fuss? You know the answer. If you don't, then ask God. The Bible says, *If any of you needs wisdom to know what you should do, you should ask God.* (James 1:5, GWT)

- Practice common sense.
- Seek your own visceral truth.
- Cultivate the wisdom of ordinariness
- Act from within.

Do you really need to know the caloric content of food products? How many servings of protein do you need daily? Do what your common sense tells you: Eat a balanced diet when you are hungry and don't stuff yourself. That is it.

Gluttony is a sin, says the Bible, and it goes on to say in one small sentence, *Your body is a temple.* (1 Cor. 6:19, GWT) So you're provided the clearest, most precise reason to avoid

transgressing against your own body. What other information do you need on diet and food when you possess such divine knowledge? Use the Bible as the rule of measure to live
your worldly life.


## BENEFIT ONLY FROM THE EXPERIENCES OF OTHER GODLY PEOPLE

*[Like] a gold ring and a fine gold ornament, [so] is constructive criti-
cism to the ear of one who listens.*

Prov. 25:12 (GWT)

In your life, from inception until now, lots of things have
happened to you. You may or may not be aware of them.
Until the age of four or five, the cortical brain is not fully
matured and can't fully register and remember what happens. But your visceral brain registers everything without
your active awareness. Don't make an effort to remember
those experiences, for their specifics may not be stored. But
the emotions that these experiences generated are registered.
And those emotions are your visceral truths.

Emotions are simple and uncomplicated realities. They
don't lie. They don't need validation by your mind. The
mind is far from simple: it lies, distorts, and conceals. Therefore, in practical living don't ask, "How do I feel about
that?" Just feel. Verbalizing the question brings your mind
in and intrudes on the visceral experience and alters it.

But visceral truth may benefit from the distilled wisdom
of previous godly generations or from the experience of
other godly people. Validate visceral truth from the enlightenment of previous generations. In your adult years, sit at
the feet of these collective spiritual experiences: they are

your sacred teachers. The ultimate validation of what you feel is right and good comes from knowing whether it is on God's side. That, of course, requires your coming of age, reaching real adulthood and knowing God. This age is the age of your spiritually steeled mind—a mind graced by God.

## GOD IS YOUR THERAPIST; REMAIN UNDER HIS CARE

> *Come to me, all who are tired from carrying heavy loads,*
> *and I will give you rest.*

> Matt. 11:28–29 (GWT)

There is no salvation of man by man. Talk to God; confide in Him. God says, *"I will instruct you. I will teach you the way that you should go. I will advise you as my eyes watch over you."* (Ps. 32:8, GWT) Talk to God anywhere. The universe is God's office and His office never closes. Talk to God as much as you want. He has unlimited time for you and His time is free of charge. A truly peaceful mind comes not from psychological knowledge, insight, or cognitive mastery over problems, but from the intuitive knowledge of God. This knowledge tames the violence of the body's innate drives, transforming them into love and compassion.

Are you searching for peace of mind? Just search for God. You aren't at the mercy of your dark unconscious. You are at the loving mercy of God. God is the best therapist. He not only understands you, He knows you. He not only listens to your problems, He knows them. If you have problems in your soul, seek peace not through some superstitious techniques but in God. He says, *"Never consult fortune-tellers."* (Lev. 19:26, GWT) *"Don't turn to psychics or mediums to get help."* (Lev. 19:31, GWT) God will provide you with a deep and hidden peace you never even knew existed. Don't look for secular salvation: it doesn't exist. Just fix your gaze on God. You can safely wobble on a well-lit road. As the psalmist sang to God, *"Your word is a lamp for my feet and a light for my path."* (Ps. 119:105, GWT)

You can talk to God silently or in a whisper or a shout. He hears everything, including the unuttered. Because God accepts you, you can tell Him anything, including your confusion, disappointment, and anger toward Him. But also listen to God. In fact, the Bible says, *We must pay closer attention to what we have heard. Then we won't drift away [from the truth].* (Heb. 2:1, GWT) All will be fine if you turn to God with your questions. He possesses the Divine Answer. The Bible says, *Be in harmony and at peace with God. In this way you will have prosperity.* (Job 22:21, GWT) *"Then God's peace, which goes beyond anything we can imagine, will guard your thoughts and emotions."* (Phil. 4:7, GWT)

## GOD IS YOUR GUIDE; STAY ON HIS WELL-BEATEN PATH

*I know the plans that I have for you.*

Jer. 29:11 (GWT)

There is a well-established myth that you can only find wisdom and enlightenment "off the beaten path." The well-beaten path is viewed as ordinary and boring. This myth is perpetuated by the metaphor of the less-used road seen as a bucolic dirt road, as compared to the littered asphalt highway of ordinary life. A better metaphor for the less-beaten path would be being lost in a dense forest.

You can compare the well-beaten path to a road leading to specific destinations. You don't have to follow a single path, but can choose from many, all with well-identified directions. The well-beaten paths to safety, joy, comfort, excitement, danger, and self-destruction have been walked on before and found to be true. Your life is a first for you, but many others have lived before you. Collective memories of the past, which you inherited with pride, and hopes for a future, which you long for with faithful hope, serve to maintain your present values. You don't need to get lost for the sake of getting lost. Therefore, ask yourself, "Where do I want to find myself?" Not many would seek the goal of self-destruction, though some may find themselves on the way to it. People who find themselves on this path either don't trust the experience of other godly people or don't heed the signposts warning of danger.

Traveling the well-beaten path (besides being safe and predictable) integrates you into your spiritual community. Deviation from it alienates you and alienation promotes further deviation. If you want to make a new path by walking in unknown territory, be sure you possess an accurate spiritual compass.

In your life you are confronted frequently with situations that require making choices. Though you may know the right thing to do and the correct path to take, you may mislead yourself by internal arguments, which pit your wishes against your reason, your fears against your defenses. You may consider the ethical, moral, and even legal implications of a choice and simultaneously try to counterbalance them with self-made wisdom and philosophy. You may list the pros and cons of intended actions and weigh and calculate the prospects. None of these elaborate schemes brings comfort or the desired result, unless the decision coincidentally aligns with your spirit. But relying on serendipity is too chancy, too complicated, and a waste of precious time.

Like all other things in life, there is an easier way. God says, *"Stand at the crossroads and look. Ask which paths are the old, reliable paths. Ask which way leads to blessings. Live that way."* (Jer. 6:16, GWT) Occasionally you may hear a different drummer, but don't ever lose sight of the bandleader.

Ask a few all-purpose questions: "Is the action that I am undertaking aligned with being godlike?" "What would God want me to do?" The Bible makes very explicit what God wants you to do: *Don't lose a minute in building on what you've been given, complementing your basic faith with good character, spiritual understanding, alert discipline, passionate patience, reverent wonder* . . . (2 Pet. 1:5–6, MSG) Once you follow that line of inquiry, you will discover a singular, valid response. It will be easy to choose the action you must take, and the result will be better than you have expected; in fact, God will deliver infinitely beyond your highest desires and thoughts.

God says, *"I have good plans for you."* (Jer. 29:11, NCV) He has good plans for your marriage, raising children, communal life and friendship, work and enjoyment. He has very good plans for all your mundane activities and for everything else from your beginning to your end, in this world and thereafter. All you have to do is just stay on His well-beaten path.

# EXERCISES FOR PSYCHO-SPIRITUAL FITNESS

### THE WISDOM LEARNED FROM THE BIBLE

*God wants me to live a responsible life.*

### MEDITATIVE EXERCISE OF SELF-REVELATION

*Have I followed the wisdom of the Bible?*

### PRAYER EXERCISE OF GRATITUDE

*Dear God, thank You for Your teachings and guidance.*

### INTENTIONAL EXERCISE OF SPIRITUAL REALIGNMENT

*I'll live the way God commanded me to live.*

*For I am not qualified to have dreams or to explain them, nor do I seek this ability or knowledge for myself, and I have concluded a pact with my Lord God that He should not send me visions or dreams or even angels. For I am content with this gift which I have, Holy Scripture, which abundantly teaches and supplies all things necessary for both this life and also for the life to come.*

Martin Luther, *Table Talk*, 1483

# CHAPTER III

# STRIVING FOR GODLY SUCCESS

*It is the LORD'S blessing that*
*makes a person rich.*

Prov. 10:22 (GWT)

When we talk about success we usually mean acquisition of wealth, power, and fame. Such accomplishments require selfish ambition that is potentially destructive and self-destructive. The Bible says, *Where you have . . . selfish ambition, there you find disorder and every evil practice.* (James 3:16, NIV)

The craving mind brings only misery. The Bible says, *A person is a slave to whatever he gives in to.* (2 Pet. 2:19, GWT) Whenever you want more money, food, clothes, sex, power, medals, or titles, you fall into the hole of wanting, and you will find yourself descending into an abyss of greed. As you purchase your thirtieth pair of shoes, thirtieth tie or dress, you propel yourself toward the next purchase. And each time you buy more things, your soul shrinks to make room for them. Insatiability is the main ingredient of greed. There is never satisfaction in craving, except in craving for spiritual salvation. The Bible says, *Desire God's pure word as new-born babies desire milk. Then you will grow in your salvation.* (1 Pet. 2:2, GWT)

Greed is a trap. Consider this example. Monkey trappers in Central Asia make a hole in the side of a hollowed coconut and tie it to a tree. Monkeys are attracted to the treat, but when a monkey puts its hand into the coconut to grab at the contents, it becomes trapped because its clenched fist is too big to pull out of the hole. Although all the monkey need do to escape is relax its fist and let go of the goods, in its greed for the treat it won't unclench its fist. The trappers can then collect their prey. The lesson of this tale is obvious: Greed can cause your demise. This is why The Bible says to *put to death whatever is worldly in you: . . . your greed* (Col. 3:5, GWT) before it puts you to death. The purpose of seeking success or wealth is to be happy, but success and wealth do not necessarily bring happiness. Nor do poverty and failure, for that matter. You can be happy or unhappy no matter what your social or economic status. Learn to be content in all situations. Say with the Bible, *I know how to live in poverty or prosperity. No matter what the situation, I've learned the secret of how to live when I'm full or when I'm hungry, when I have too much or when I have too little.* (Phil. 4:12, GWT) So, what is that secret?

Wanting what you already have is the secret to happiness. If your measure of success is primarily accumulative in nature, you will not find happiness. Acquiring more of anything becomes cumbersome and cluttering, and more significantly, is self-perpetuating. It will weigh you down. Whatever satisfaction comes with "having" lasts briefly, leaving you feeling emptier than before your latest acquisition. "More" digs a bigger hole in the psyche, so that wanting becomes an insatiable desire. This is especially true for money. The Bible says, *Whoever loves money will never be satisfied with money. Whoever loves wealth will never be satisfied with more income.* (Eccles. 5:10, GWT)

Those who have money, power, and fame may seem to "have it all." However, those who have it all rarely are satisfied because there is no "all" when it comes to money, power, and fame. There is always more to have, and as long as there's more to have, there will be no contentment. The accumulation of anything is addictive and all addictions are insatiable. These addicted people are haunted by the vague sense of discomfort of having missed opportunities. There is no place to rest. There is no place to arrive. The acquisition of things and satisfaction and true happiness are measured on different, if not opposite, scales.

Happiness and prosperity are obtained *not* from having an abundance of things—not from overfeeding the ego, but rather from underfeeding it. The less you have on your plate (metaphorically and literally), the more space your soul has to expand, and to be nourished and enriched by its expansion. Real prosperity is the abundance of spiritual thoughts and deeds.

While satisfaction—material fullness—correlates with accumulative appropriation, happiness—spiritual fullness—correlates with disappropriation, with giving away. Fullness will flow into you in the measure you become empty. The Bible says, *If you give, you will receive. Your gift will return to you in full measure, pressed down, shaken together to make room for more, and running over. Whatever measure you use in giving—large or small—it will be used to measure what is given back to you.* (Luke 6:38, NLT)

Happiness is a state that you reach by subtraction. It is wishing for what you have and still emptying out, a joyful disappropriation. Happiness is the feeling of owning everything while possessing nothing. It is in the Bible: *People think we are sad although we're always glad, that we're beggars although we make many people spiritually rich, that we have nothing although we possess everything.* (2 Cor. 6:10, GWT)

## WEALTH AND POWER ARE NOT UNHOLY, BUT THE LOVE OF THEM IS

*If a man cleanses himself from the latter [ignoble purposes],*
*he will be an instrument for noble purposes, made holy.*

2 Tim. 2:21 (NIV)

For some people the stock market is akin to the Day of Judgment, offering condemnation or redemption. Such judgment, if you allow it to, can break your spiritual backbone: you begin relating to other people (and even to yourself) as a commodity. If you lose the "I—Thou" relationship, converting to "I—It," you simply will manipulate others and use every available instrument to dominate and shape friends, family, and coworkers into becoming whom you desire them to be. This perversion may even convince some people to give up their identities and accept the roles assigned by the manipulator.

The Bible says, *Whoever loves wealth is never satisfied with his income. This too is meaningless.* (Eccles. 5:10, NIV-UK) This meaninglessness takes the form of a frantic existence in which unholy people pursue their goals by every means available (including ethically and legally questionable ones). They consider cheating, lying, and deceiving as legitimate means of pursuing their goals. They will betray friends, colleagues, and even members of their own families. For them there are no permanent friends, only permanent interests— their own. But sooner or later their deceptive practices are revealed, and such unholy people become abhorred. No one "delights" in their works, no matter how impressive their accomplishments or how generous the use of their wealth. The Bible says, *Dishonest scales are disgusting to the LORD, but accurate weights are pleasing to him.* (Prov. 11:1, GWT)

- Empty out.
- Joyfully disappropriate.
- Eliminate vices.
- Wish for what you have.

Those with unholy purposes are relatively free from anxiety because they feel no sense of guilt and shame. They become anxious only if threatened, such as when found guilty in a legal sense. As soon as the threat dissipates, they continue the questionable behavior. They believe only in the impersonal imperatives of profit. This nihilism generates self-corrupting aimlessness and an inner lawlessness. The best-known of these people are featured regularly in scandals reported in the business section of newspapers. One unscrupulous man had the audacity to misuse a biblical quotation as an explanation for his predatory business behavior: *Be as cunning as snakes.* (Matt. 10:16, GWT)

Unholy purposes are devotions without virtue: they are fueled by furious passions, vile excesses, and frenzied pursuits. Those who pursue unholy purposes experience (at best) a counterfeit ecstasy in the worship of their goals and themselves. What they experience is a perversion of the soul, an uneasiness of mind, a privation of good, all of which culminate in the stagnancy of the spirit. Acquiring anything near their goal, which is itself a moving target, does not bring gratification to those with unholy purposes, but only echoes their core unhappiness.

The unholy person cannot escape three abysses:

1. Loss of money, power, and fame
2. Being given a taste of his or her own medicine by friends, colleagues, and members of the family; i.e., being treated as a commodity
3. Facing death

The first abyss, bankruptcy of potency, is devastating when it occurs because unholy people equate their worth with money, power, and fame. The loss equals a loss of self. The unholy person's self is not a real self, but a counterfeit one. His losses expose his outer lies and his inner truth: an empty hole that quickly fills with illnesses, addictions, and destructive and self-destructive behavior.

The second abyss, emotional bankruptcy, involves emotional isolation and lovelessness. Relationships bring no joy, honesty, or genuine love, as friends, colleagues, and even intimates treat unholy people as they were treated—as an article of trade. The Bible couldn't make it clearer: *I'm bankrupt without love.* (1 Cor. 13:3, MSG)

The third abyss, spiritual bankruptcy, takes its harshest toll at the time of dying and is truly frightening. When facing death, unholy people walk into a dark hole of oblivion. Their possessions, power, and wealth cannot prevent death; as an old proverb goes, "A shroud has no pockets." Everything you think you own is lent temporarily for your use and safekeeping, to be passed along to the next recipient. The world and all that is in it belongs to God. The Bible says, *To you, O God, belong[s]. . . . everything in heaven, everything on earth.* (1 Chron. 29:11, MSG) This is not an order for deprivation; it is a lesson about eternity.

## YOUR SUCCESS DEPENDS ON PROTECTING YOUR GROUND

*A little yeast spreads through the whole batch of dough.*

Gal. 5:9 (GWT)

You are entitled to your own fullest growth—to strive to win, to succeed, and even to be zealous. But God permits only holy ambitions. The Bible says, *It is fine to be zealous, provided the purpose is good.* (Gal. 4:18, NIV) One way of securing the goodness of your purpose is protecting the very ground that assures your success, if not your survival. If you gain by depleting the ground beneath you, eventually you will lose. Power and wealth bring happiness only when used to serve others. As you ascend to your ambitions, you have to devote equal attention to the well-being of the ground from which you spring: your firm, company, profession, business, and community. You can grow only if your community remains healthy and enables others to grow. The Bible tells us, *As each part does its own special work, it helps the other parts grow, so that the whole body is healthy.* (Eph. 4:16, NLT) If you are the only one who emerges as a functioning part while the whole fails, your own future will be endangered.

- Help others without expecting reciprocity.
- Be generous without expecting gratitude.
- Sacrifice your interests for the good of the whole.
- Don't brag about your successes.

Thinking you're the center of your own world is a human, forgivable trait; trying to be the center of the world, however, is a sin to which unholy people succumb. Being a holy person requires self-sacrifice, which, in itself, has its own reward. Self-sacrifice fulfills personal interest by negating it. Sacrifice humbles the body and pursues the elimination of vices, no matter how tempting the vice. Self-sacrifice is the rejection of a selfish life; it humbles the ego and pursues the elimination of pride and greed, no matter how tempting it might be to be proud and greedy.

The ultimate success is to live your life in a way that will enable you to feel free of guilt and absent of remorse when you reach the end of your journey. Success means living a virtuous life, a godly life, not only in the personal but also in the professional arena. This requires cultivating the Holy Purpose. It is only through the gate of faithful purpose that all virtues enter. Good exists only with God. Freedom from God, which some misdirected "philosophers of self" promote, is not freedom. It is the loss of goodness, the source of godlikeness. There can be no joyful success without God. Success without God may bring pleasures to one's self while bringing suffering to others. God demands self-sacrifice for the good of the community, and this type of sacrifice brings godly joy to you as it ends the suffering of others.

Money is said to be a good servant but a bad master. If you use money and power in a self-serving, predatory fashion, they corrode your soul. On the other hand, if you use them altruistically, putting them in the service of a meaningful mission, they will enrich your soul. What the Bible says about the gift of healing is true for every thing: *Give these things without charging, since you received them without paying.* (Matt. 10:8, GWT)

If you believe that you come into the world with nothing and that you'll leave with nothing, you can give away everything you own while you are alive. Give away not only your money, but also your time and energy. Using your resources to serve others is the surest way to find happiness and prosperity. The most difficult hurdle you will encounter on the road to happiness is the leap from self-centeredness—self-interest—to other-centeredness. The Bible says, *Each of you should look not only to your own interests, but also to the interests of others.* (Phil. 2:4, NIV) There, you will not only be happier, but also even richer. The Bible says: *The generous man will be prosperous.* (Prov. 11:25, NASB)

# EXERCISES FOR PSYCHO-SPIRITUAL FITNESS

### THE WISDOM LEARNED FROM THE BIBLE

*God wants me not to pursue selfish ambitions*

### MEDITATIVE EXERCISE OF SELF-REVELATION

*Have I been too greedy, too self-centered?*

### PRAYER EXERCISE OF GRATITUDE

*Dear God, thank You for Your spiritual milk.*

### INTENTIONAL EXERCISE OF SPIRITUAL REALIGNMENT

*I will self-sacrifice more
for the good of the whole.*

## MEANING IS INHERENT IN ALL WORK

*Faith by itself is dead if it doesn't cause you to do any good things.*

James 2:17 (GWT)

We have a tendency to divide work into the categories of meaningful versus meaningless. How do we arrive at these conclusions? Is being a nurse more meaningful than driving a taxi? Is managing a store more meaningful than being a gardener? Is being a homebuilder more meaningful than being a homemaker? Who decides? What are the criteria? We differentiate jobs based on their desirability, prestige, and financial rewards. Do we confuse these things with meaningfulness? When you're in pain, a doctor or a dentist is invaluable; but if you are hungry, they are useless. An architect may loom large in your eyes when designing and building your house, but he isn't going to take care of the house afterward. You'll need a housekeeper for that. There is no such thing as meaningless work. There is work that is easier or more difficult, less- or better-compensated, and there are occupations that are stressful or enjoyable.

You may be bored with your job; you may feel exploited and mistreated. This is not because the work is meaningless. You may have a difficult boss; you may not be fit for the job, lacking the skills or aptitude required; or you may be unhappy for reasons unrelated to the job. The work itself, however, is not meaningless. I have seen men working at the fish market show camaraderie toward other workers as they clean the catch with gusto. I've noticed orderlies sweeping the floors of an operating room, gathering bloody tissues, bandages, and pads with singular attention. I've observed a kind, elderly doorman's devotion to the comfort and safety of the tenants in his care. These people were hardworking individuals who didn't question whether their jobs were meaningful or not. It is a matter how of you look at it. If you change the way you view a thing, the thing changes.

You need to view things from the perspective of godliness. Is the work you are engaged in directed toward a Holy Purpose? If not, your work conditions will only compound the problem and prevent you from doing good work. You need to disengage from all unholy purposes in order to succeed. The Bible says, *If a man cleanses himself from [ignoble purposes], he will be an instrument for noble purposes, made holy, useful to the Master and prepared to do any good work.* (2 Tim. 2:21, NIV)

Meaning is inherent in all work, but you have to extract meaning from it. There are three conditions that you must meet for the successful extraction of meaning from your job.

- First, you have to know yourself. You can't know what you want to do if you don't know yourself.
- Second, you have to evaluate realistically your circumstances to make sure they support what you want to do.
- Third, if the previous two conditions are in place, you must devote all your attention, energy, and enthusiasm to the job. Lean forward wholeheartedly and work as if everything about the job depends on you.

The Bible says, *Make a careful exploration of who you are and the work you have been given, and then sink yourself into that.* (Gal. 6:4, MSG)

- Estimate your abilities correctly.
- Become competent.
- Be imaginative and creative.
- Work with attention and enthusiasm.

In Chapter I we discussed how to know yourself: by knowing God. Once you know God, you'll know *who* you are, and you can move to the other two conditions.

The second condition, realistically evaluating your circumstances, is related primarily to your competence in or predisposition for a particular type of work and your determination to pursue it.

As the potter shapes clay, you need to shape yourself. God has given you to you. You are your own clay and potter. Becoming is not passive; committing yourself requires a spiritual activism. You have to assess your aptitudes and then make your choice. But your perception of yourself may not correspond exactly with your strengths. You need to align your desire with your competence and focus on bringing them together. You have to choose what you can harvest before you can plant the crop. The Bible tells us, *Try to have a sane estimate of your capabilities.* (Rom. 12:3, Ph) Then learn a trade—no matter how simple or complex—and become very good at it. "It" can be teaching children, cooking, managing a store, driving a bus, playing a musical instrument, ministering—anything. The Bible says, *Be sure to use the gift God gave you.* (1 Tim 4:14, NLV)

If you follow the Bible's instructions, you are halfway to finding meaning in your work. But if you aren't good at whatever you're doing, you won't find meaning in doing it. Inability and incompetence breed discontent, frustration, anger (directed at yourself and others), and disengagement.

Competence is the basic requirement for finding the meaning inherent in work. But the depth of meaning multiplies if you go beyond delivering routine competency and infuse yourself with what you are doing. That means fully engaging and sprinkling your creative juices over your work: You can improve a beef stew competently prepared from a recipe by improvising with different vegetables; perk up plain kitchen floor tiles by interspersing tiles of a different design and color; enliven a class by inviting guest speakers.

Now comes the third condition. Once you've found yourself, then evaluated your disposition and gained competence, you are ready to extract the full meaning from your work. The depth of meaning you extract from your own work corresponds to the degree of orderly attention you direct into it. The Bible tells us, *Everything must be done in a proper and orderly way.* (1 Cor. 14:40, GWT) Give even the most repetitive tasks the same degree of attention you did when you first carried them out. Such attention and full engagement draws you to discover new details of the work, adds greater accuracy to the results, and imparts job satisfaction. Full engagement means total devotion to the activity in which you are involved, whether the project lasts for hours or years. A scribbled life doesn't engage the spirit. Whatever you are doing right now, give it your total attention. A student asked a wise man for some words of wisdom about success. "Attention," replied the man. The student was not satisfied and asked the master to elaborate. The master complied and said: "Attention, attention."

Singular attention is obtained by enthusiasm. Enthusiasm describes devotional commitment and engagement. The Bible urges, *Whatever you do, do it wholeheartedly as though you were working for your real master and not merely for humans.* (Col. 3:23, GWT) Once you get there, you are no longer simply doing the work: your work is an extension of yourself. You are created and you create. You may create food, furniture, clothes, or books, or you may provide service for what has been created, through cleaning, organizing, deposing, safekeeping, or transporting it. Although your signature may not be visible in the corner of your work, your fingerprints will be all over it, imbedded in the fingerprints of God.

## WORK IS JOY

*Be sure to do what you should, for then you will enjoy*
*the personal satisfaction of having done your work well.*

Gal. 6:4 (NLT)

After a long, hard day of work you want to come home to relax, enjoy your family, share the day's events with each other, have dinner and settle down to watch a television show or listen to music. On weekends you attend congregational meetings, visit friends, play games or watch your children play games. All these after-work activities are wonderful and well deserved, provided they do not become your primary goals.

Work shouldn't be an activity you tolerate so that you can get back to your leisure life. You should look forward to going to work as much as you do to going home. Your perspective has to do with how engaged you are in your work.

Why is selling real cars to real people less interesting than watching a reality show? Why is working as a nurse in the hospital less interesting than watching a medical drama on television? It's the actors' engagement in their work that makes those shows interesting; actors who aren't engaged or engaging can sink a well-scripted show. No job is uninteresting, no matter how dull it may sound. There are only uninterested people.

Furthermore, seeing your work as something "to get over with" makes leisure time activities loom large, and they take on too much importance and value in your life. Ironically, these coveted leisure activities always end up disappointing you. Yet increasing leisure time to find greater satisfaction only makes things worse. You probably have heard people saying they need a vacation after returning from "fun-filled" time off.

Obviously, leisure activities are different from work. But if you find something likeable in your work, you can get pleasure from it. A secretary told me, "I like going to work and spending time with my co-worker and friend, Jane. I just enjoy sitting next to her." A jeweler said, "I open the shop every morning. Putting the key in the lock and turning it and knowing that it will open gives me immense pleasure. There I am, alone in the middle of the shop. All these boxes are waiting for me to open them and put their contents in the window. I know where each piece of jewelry belongs. I touch each of them, one by one. They shine on me and I nod to them." Finding pleasure at work will balance your excessive expectations of your spouse, friends, and children at the end of the day or workweek.

Somehow our culture began to associate work with the chore of making a living, something we have to do, something we must endure and finish each day with as little effort and time as possible—and not something to look forward to or value or even to enjoy. We overvalue leisure time; we can scarcely wait to get home. TGIF (Thank God It's Friday) has become a common sentiment, reflecting the work-versus-pleasure dichotomy. People use different rationales to justify their disengagement from their jobs: Why put my heart into my work, since we are all exploited by rich capitalists? I don't work hard because I don't like my job. Life is too short to take the job seriously; I like to have idle time, fun, and joy in life.

But too much leisure time doesn't necessarily bring fun and joy. If anything it draws out the bodily desires, demanding great restraint, and it frequently brings trouble. A proverb says, "The devil tempts all, but the idle man tempts the devil."

If pleasure becomes associated only with leisure activities, work is relegated to the boring zone. That distinction—pleasure versus boredom—is an artificial setup, projecting inner unhappiness onto the most convenient external scapegoat: work. In fact, those who are unhappy at work aren't that much fun at home or on the playground either. They tend to be disengaged from whatever they do.

Happiness comes only through full engagement, whether at leisure activity or work. The nature of your work and where you do it is secondary to being committed to it. Make your work one of your missions in life—"dipping your bread in your sweat," as the old saying goes. Carry out your duties with full acceptance and devotion and you'll find a profound joy above and beyond simple happiness. No matter how small the job or how mundane it may seem, if it is done with utmost care and attention, the job will bring a sacred pleasure unattainable by any kind of leisure activity.

## WORK IS SACRED

*Whoever wants to become great among you will be your servant.*

Mark 10:43 (GWT)

The sacredness of work is not an abstract concept. It is not sufficient to be a competent and enthusiastic servant of God; you also must be a humble and trustworthy servant. The Bible says, *You must serve each other with humility.* (1 Pet. 5:5, GWT) It also warns us to be trustworthy in whatever we do, even if it is a minor task. *Whoever can be trusted with very little can also be trusted with a lot. Whoever is dishonest with very little is dishonest with a lot.* (Luke 16:10, GWT)

There is nothing inherently wrong in being proud of your work. But crowning yourself with pride is self-idolatry, the chain of the spirit. God demands (and everyone appreciates) modesty. The Bible puts it in starkest terms: *I won't brag about myself, unless it is about my weaknesses.* (2 Cor. 12:5, GWT) Pride is an unholy state. You cannot even be proud of not being proud. God also cautions us against excessive self-confidence; the Bible warns: *Don't be so . . . self-confident. You're not exempt. You could fall flat on your face as easily as anyone else.* (1 Cor. 10:12, MSG)

There is also nothing wrong in expecting appreciation and reward for your work. Remember, though, there is a difference between a reward and merit for a job. A reward is what you may receive from others in compensation for the work, while merit is what you earn from doing the work itself. If you work only for recognition in the eyes of another person, the focus shifts from the work to the judgment of that person. The approval or disapproval of that person (or the potential reward that accompanies it) becomes your main point of reference and limits your imaginative power and creativity. More important, if you make someone else the point of reference for your work's value, you'll never be able to value the work for itself.

The sacred nature of work is best preserved when it is true in itself. Such work more than pleases everyone, even the most difficult employer, because it brings with it the air of authenticity—its true merit.

You might ask: "Should I commit to any work or only to specific tasks?" My answer is that under optimal conditions people can learn and commit themselves to any type of work. The Bible says, *If you wait for perfect conditions, you'll never get anything done.* (Eccles. 11:4, NLT) If you plant, you'll harvest, even if you were not a farmer in your heart. But the fullest commitment, with corresponding creativity and productivity, is best obtained if the work resonates with your soul. There is no doubt that temperament, innate talent, and even brain structure predispose people toward certain occupations. But these are only predispositions. Like bees that can make honey from every flower, you can be a success in every job. Honey made from different flowers will have variations in color, taste, and smell, but all are very similar in nutritional value. Similarly the results of your work will vary, but you will have the same feeling of internal satisfaction, provided you work like a bee—relentlessly, determinedly, enthusiastically, steadily, and with singular attention, day after day, year after year.

If you define success by external criteria, you remain chronically anxious because life circumstances are utterly unpredictable. External goals demand enormous effort, and because the focus on them changes as you near achieving them, they always remain distant. But if success is defined by internal criteria—full commitment to the love of work— you'll be at peace. Such success doesn't depend on factors you cannot control; it depends on a factor over which you have full control: your attitude toward work. The internal goal is effortless; once achieved, the focus remains fixed, and therefore, the goal is always near. To be successful in your work, learn to identify with it. Then the work becomes not something you do but another manifestation of who you are. The Bible says, *You can tell what they are by what they do.* (Matt. 7:16, CEV) The work itself becomes the point of reference for success or failure, which no longer depends on the promise of reward or threat of punishment. The love you extend to your work returns as self-confidence, self-appreciation, self-recognition, and self-worth—the ultimate success.

## YOUR PERSONAL GOALS MUST REFLECT YOUR INNER SELF AND BE ALIGNED WITH GOD'S WISHES

*I run straight toward the goal.*

Phil. 3:14 (GWT)

Your actions are either responses to demands of outside forces or are generated from within yourself. Of course, there is a mixture of these two that operates within any given situation. If, in life, you act primarily as a reactor or perform a role assigned to you by others, your soul will gradually shrivel. Your assignments may range from a role in the family to a role in the community: "You are a listener." "You are an entertainer." "You are an audience." "You pick up after the mess of any sort." "You fill gaps." "You do chores." These actions may or may not be suitable for or desirable to you. None of these roles is inherently good or bad. The question is: do they reflect your inner self? Your actions should resonate within your soul. If they don't, you are not living a full life.

Your role, your actions, your outer self should reflect your inner self. Then, in full harmony with your outer and inner self, you'll replenish your soul with every action you take, regardless of how important or unimportant the action might be. When your soul is reflected through the prism of your actions, it will convey your sincerity and commitment. Your actions become an extension of your authentic self. You won't be acting a designated role but enacting yourself in a given context. The enacting from within will keep you focused on your goal.

Single-minded focusing, unaligned with your soul and God's wishes, brings results but not necessarily healthy ones. A determined attitude to marry someone, to take over a business, to get a certain award, to buy something, or even to get pregnant or adopt a child may succeed. If the goal is not fully aligned with your soul, immediately after you achieve your goal you will be only temporarily and relatively satisfied (if not mildly depressed). To get what you so badly want will create mixed feelings once you achieve it. You can't remain joyfully serene because the energy used in focusing on that specific goal will not be self-regenerative.

You need to focus to achieve your earthly goal, but that goal has to be aligned with your soul and with God. The Bible says you need to *unite all things in him, things in heaven and things on earth.* (Eph.1:10, ESV)

Those who love their work do not work for the eyes of other people, but for the eyes of God. A worker with such commitment is like the medieval artisans who carved the backs of statues with the same skill, attention, and loyalty that the master sculptors applied to carving the fronts of the statues. These unnamed artisans knew that though no human eyes would see their work because it would fit snugly against a wall, God's eyes would. That is the meaning of work's being true in and of itself—it is done for God's eyes. When your overarching goal—working for God—is so clearly identified, the steps that you must take to bring the goal about will be laid before you. You will *run straight to the goal with purpose in every step.* (1 Cor. 9:26, NLT)

## THE HOLY COMMITMENT AND DETERMINATION BRING SUCCESS

*Plant your seeds in the morning, and do not be lazy in the evening. You do not know which will grow well, the morning or evening planting, or if both of them alike will do well.*

Eccles. 11:6 (NLV)

"Why didn't I succeed?" asked a young sales agent who was passed over for a promotion after being on the job for a year and a half. "I am as creative and as smart as the next guy. I had a good education, I'm reasonably good-looking, I'm a pleasant and friendly person. Did I pick the wrong field for myself? Was I too cautious in approaching customers?" Maybe. In fact, the Bible answers that last specific point: *Whoever watches the wind will never plant. Whoever looks at the clouds will never harvest.* (Eccles. 11:4, GWT)

- Bring reverence to your work.
- Every day learn more.
- Make success out of failures.
- Work with a smile on your face.

All the qualities that the salesman has cited, including excessive cautiousness, are only relative contributors to lack of success. So are the many other factors such as lack of education or physical stamina. The primary contributors to failure are lack of commitment and the incompetence that derives from it. Unsuccessful people lack commitment. Competence doesn't occur in a vacuum; it's not an inherited trait, such as having blue eyes or being tall. Competence is the result of working hard with a full commitment to getting better at the job.

What are the distinguishing qualities of totally engaged people? Fully committed people bring spiritual intent and reverence to all work to which they are called. God doesn't differentiate the sacred from the secular. Everything is sacred. People who fully engage in their work weave the sacred into their labors, including the ordinary chores of life.

One way of knowing whether you have evolved to have faith is to check how much effort it takes you to do your work. There may be some realignment needed, if, at the end of the day, you are exhausted by a job that is within the level of your competence and skills.

Failures at all levels of competence and capabilities are related to lack of whole-hearted commitment to the task at hand. God tells us, *"By the sweat of your brow, you will produce food to eat."* (Gen. 3:19, GWT) This verse always reminds me of a young man I once knew. The youngster languished from chronic inertia. Whenever I suggested an activity to him, he replied with, "I'll try." Don't try! Just do it!

Trying is a tentativeness that commonly causes failure. Commitment means believing in the purpose of the task, understanding its nature, and transforming yourself into a native of the endeavor. Once fully engaged, you will harness yourself to the task and concentrate with singular attention to bringing about the desired result. A fully committed person finds a creative solution to almost any task.

There is an ancient fable of a king who fell off his horse and found that in his fall he had cracked his favorite diamond pendant. He consulted the finest jewelers in the land and all agreed that nothing could be done to repair the gem whose crack now ran down its center. Suddenly one old jeweler stepped forward, proclaiming he could fix the stone within a month. Reluctantly the king gave the diamond to the old jeweler and declared that should the jeweler fail after making such an arrogant promise, he would pay for his hubris with his hands.

The old man took the diamond and left. Exactly one month later he returned with the diamond pendant inside a box. The king opened the box and examined the jewel. The crack was still there. Enraged, the king ordered his guard to cut off the jeweler's hands. As the jeweler was being dragged away he yelled, "Please, Your Majesty, turn the diamond over!" The king turned over the pendant. There, at the top of the stone was a rose; the crack was its stem.

Commitment means steadiness: no one succeeds overnight. Most accomplishments are less the outcome of brilliant minds and more the determination of strong-willed individuals.

Failures do not occur overnight either. They tend to reflect a lack of determination over a period of time.

Should failures occur, independent of your total commitment, get up, dust yourself off, and reengage. Your past is not your future. Full commitment comes with optimism and self-confidence, and such devotional engagement uplifts the spirit. If you fall with a smile and pick yourself up still smiling, you have not failed; you just didn't succeed at that specific task. Even if, despite of all your best efforts, you keep failing at a specific task, you still are succeeding at confirming your determination and strengthening your will. You gain accumulated experiences from repeated failure by learning how to recover from failure. With each recovery you will accumulate a repertoire of survival skills and gain greater self-confidence. You'll realize you haven't failed at all. In fact, you've succeeded in a much broader sense, far beyond what you might have gained by succeeding in that particular matter.

# EXERCISES FOR PSYCHO-SPIRITUAL FITNESS

### THE WISDOM LEARNED FROM THE BIBLE

*God wants me to sink myself into the work
I have been given.*

### MEDITATIVE EXERCISE OF SELF-REFLECTION

*Have I been fully committed to my work?*

### PRAYER EXERCISE OF GRATITUDE

*Dear God, thank You for the work
You have given me.*

### INTENTIONAL EXERCISE
OF SPIRITUAL ALIGNMENT.

*I'll put all my attention and enthusiasm
into my work.*

## YOUR LIMITATIONS ARE YOUR REALITIES AND ALSO YOUR POTENTIAL

*Keep on growing in your knowledge.*

Phil. 1:9 (NLT)

We all are limited in one way or another. Don't define yourself, however, by your limitations. A great surgeon may be utterly useless on a basketball court, a competent advertising agent probably can't fix an electrical short circuit, a talented money manager may not be able to contain a kindergarten class, and a gifted artist may not know how to operate a videocassette recorder. But you must have the right perspective on limitations. We tend to think negatively, to focus on our limitations and to elaborate on their undesirable consequences. If you keep doing this, eventually you will become depressed and feel like a failure. If you look at anyone from a generally negative point of view, you'll see everyone is a relative failure. In reality, everyone can be a success at something. How? By learning, exploring, and experiencing.

The best learning comes from experience. You may read a lot about driving, but until you sit behind the wheel of a car you can't understand what it's like to drive. You may be informed about the dangers of driving too fast but until you have a brush with a near-accident, all that caution applies to others and not to you. Similarly everything we read and listen to in schools and elsewhere about life is merely theoretical information until we encounter it in the real world. The lessons, whether about computers or cooking or sewing, eventually must be practiced and the information converted to experience. You need to gain experiences in order to navigate in life—even though at times you may not feel up to them. Inactivity will close the door on opportunities. On the other hand when you take action, you may find that "feeling up for it" will open doors for other opportunities.

This doesn't mean you should be chasing rainbows. Have realistic expectations of yourself—you can miss either by aiming too high or too low, as the old saying goes—then put those expectations into action. However, you should never go against your nature. There is a story of a fish that wanted to learn to live on land. Every day the fish practiced staying out of the water, remaining on the grass by the water's edge for longer and longer periods. After many months the fish didn't need to go back into the water at all. The fish moved inland and was pleased with its new life. Then one day a driving rain flooded the land. The fish drowned.

Don't let your wishes and fantasies exceed reality or you may end up drowning in them. Make sure your enthusiasm is matched by your realistic actions. The Bible says, *Now finish doing it also, so that just as there was the readiness to desire it, so there may be also the completion of it by your ability.* (2 Cor. 8:11, NASB)

Sit down and identify your current skills and qualities, and your potential skills and the chances of your actualizing them. *God in his kindness gave each of us different gifts.* (Rom. 12:6, GWT) Ask your intimates or spiritual friends for an honest evaluation of your conclusions. Convey your determination to them, then listen to their opinions without being hurt or flattered. Your present skills are your baseline strengths. Make the best of these qualities regardless of how short they may fall compared to your potential; they are the proverbial "bird in the hand," be they farming, managing, or selling. Then do your best to actualize your potentials.

- Be true to your work.
- Make a full commitment.
- Work for its merit.
- Serve with humility.

It is equally important not to stifle your dreams, though on the surface they may seem unsuitable for your temperament. Share your wishes and fantasies with your friends and intimates, but don't ask for any feedback, validation, or negation. Just share your wishes as they are. Make your fantasies and related aspirations your hobbies. If, for example, you are a music teacher, you may fantasize about recording popular songs or composing a musical score. Go ahead! But don't make it a preoccupation or the exclusive goal of your life, to the point where you lose your zest for teaching. Try to become the best music teacher in your school as a way of actualizing your best potential.

Mastery is an eternal apprenticeship from which you never graduate. For a true master, the satisfaction drawn from the feeling of having arrived pales in comparison to having open-ended access to learning. At best the "arrived" feeling in a profession generates a false sense of security. More important, it stagnates a person. Make a habit of learning something every day, even if it's not in your own field. Don't you occasionally hear something unrelated to your interests or your work that intrigues you? Your face brightens with wonder: "Steel is iron alloyed with a small amount of carbon? I didn't know that!" It isn't the sense of arrival but the sense of wonderment that is the ultimate mastery.

Some people think that doggedly following a dream is an admirable quality. It is, if there is a genuine potential. If not, such a single-minded, semi-delusional pursuit may become self-destructive because it is a form of greed. Be grateful for the skills God gave you; He says, *"I will instruct you. I will teach you the way that you should go."* (Ps. 32:8, GWT) Nevertheless, this doesn't mean letting your limitations define you.

"I'm not good in math" a student told me, "I can't even balance my checkbook. I am just not smart, period." It may be true that this student wasn't good in math and that he couldn't balance his checkbook, but escalating that fact to the generalized statement "I am not smart" was wrong and dispiriting. There are different types of intelligence, such as quantitative, qualitative, perceptual, conceptual, emotional, social, and more. You may not be good in mathematical science but you may be very good in the social sciences. You might not be able to decipher a balance sheet but you might run a meeting well. Your eyes may glaze when you have to read a position paper but you may be sharp-witted during an interview. Interestingly enough, people who have high social and emotional abilities often don't consider themselves smart. You don't hear anyone say, "I relate well to people: I am a genius!"

Identifying your limitation with your self is the equivalent of inflicting self-injury. Besides being wrong, these generalizations—"I am dumb, I am inept"—are a self-fulfilling prophecy. Of course, you must identify your *genuine* limitations and attempt to remedy or to come to terms with them.

Spiritual engagement in your work should not cloud your ability to judge your capacity to deliver. An old adage reminds us that if you stretch a bow to its very fullest, you'll wish you had stopped before it snapped. Even the most spiritual people have limitations.

Don't use others as the point of reference by which you measure yourself. That is the surest way to feel insecure and envious. There are always people who may be more gifted than you are. Insecurity and envy are poisonous to your soul. These feelings generate negative energy. Once caught in their snare you'll be proud of neither your work nor yourself. But if you do your best at what you are good at, you'll be proud of it. Your work is its own point of reference. The Bible says, *Be proud of your own accomplishments without comparing yourself to others.* (Gal. 6:4, GWT) You can compare your work with previous tasks you've done. Try good-heartedly to outdo yourself, but only yourself.

# EXERCISES FOR PSYCHO-SPIRITUAL FITNESS

## THE WISDOM LEARNED FROM THE BIBLE

*God wants me to grow in knowledge.*

## MEDITATIVE EXERCISE OF SELF-REVELATION

*Have I been aware of my limitations and how to remedy them?*

## PRAYER EXERCISE OF GRATITUDE

*Dear God, thank You for my lessons.*

## INTENTIONAL EXERCISE OF SPIRITUAL REALIGNMENT

*Today I'll learn something.*

# IF YOU RODE ON THE BACKS OF OTHERS, CARRY THEM NOW

*God has . . . created us for a life of good deeds.*

Eph. 2:10 (GNT)

There is a parable of a man whose wife had been captured by a king and brought to his castle as a slave. The man set off with his five-year-old son to rescue the woman. During their arduous trip the father had to carry his son because the boy was too young and too small to walk all the way. Finally, the two arrived at the castle. The castle gate was closed, but there was a small, narrow window in the wall alongside the gate. The boy realized that he was small enough to fit through the window; he climbed up the wall and through the window and opened the gate for his father.

We all need each other. Living a life without ever needing someone, using someone, or being used by someone is rare. If you're a fair person, usually you will find an equitable solution; however, you may not always be able to find one. You may end up employing others' talents. There, at least you should be generous. God tells us to be charitable toward our employees. *Never muzzle an ox while it is threshing grain.* (Deut. 25:4, GWT) People resent "being ridden." Even the best and most merciful rider is still the rider. But such relationships are inevitable in a society. Soldiers fight, generals get stars; research associates discover, professors get promoted; salesmen move merchandise, CEO's receive large bonuses. Of course, it is likely that at one time you carried others: once, you were a soldier, a research associate, or a salesman. Hopefully, you were used for good causes.

God permits that: *Be used for righteous purposes.* (Rom. 6:13, GNT)

Contribution from one generation to another is fine, but not sufficient. You must also deliver now. You must take care of your soldiers, associates, and salesmen if and when you become the rider. Compensate them financially, share your glory, recognize their efforts in your success or help them in other ways. This is not totally charitable or altruistic behavior. In a larger arena you may still need help and perhaps you'll receive it from totally unexpected sources. The Bible says, *Those who help others are helped.* (Prov. 11:25, MSG)

Riding others may be inevitable but the rider and the ridden must safely arrive at their destination together. You may not be able to carry the ones who carried you, but think of their souls as an extension of yours and show an equal degree of attention and interest in their souls. Jobs may be defined differently in any system, but each is unique in its contribution to the overall mission.

## A SMILE IS A SIGN OF GRATITUDE

*Be joyful!*

Phil. 4:4 (GWT)

Look around you. Everything in your sight has been built, planted, and organized for your use and benefit. And I don't mean the indispensables of living, such as air and water, which God offers for free. I mean the buildings in which you live or work; the roads on which you travel; the trees whose fruit you eat; the schools, libraries, museums, universities, and theaters you enjoy. People who lie mostly forgotten in unvisited tombs made these wonderful things. You benefit from their hard work. In their anonymity, they were the hands and feet of God. You may be part of this sacred history by doing God's work for future generations. Be grateful for the opportunity to be useful as an instrument of His deeds.

Being useful is the cornerstone of the meaning of life, and work is the concrete manifestation of such usefulness. However, to extract meaning from work you must be grateful for having work, for being able to work, for having loving coworkers and knowing that you are contributing something to the world. This recognition, if you allow it, will bring a smile to your face. Keep your energy system high by thinking beautiful thoughts; they'll also make you beautiful. Gratefulness is the ultimate prosperity. With your positive attitude you'll make others feel joyful and you'll deserve one of the greatest blessings of God: His smile. There is a prayer in the Bible, *The LORD will smile on you and be kind to you.* (Num. 6:25, GWT)

Those who wear an angry, irritable, and depressed face at work, whatever the justification, are suffering from a lack of gratitude. They can find meaning neither in their work nor elsewhere in their lives. Their mood at work carries to their home life and everywhere else, including their sleep. Nothing makes any difference to these negative people—no increase in salary, no promotion, no change of job—though they claim it might. After a short respite following such an external gratification, they'll return to their ungrateful mode. Don't allow their negative emotions—irritation, weariness, boredom, feelings of worthlessness—to get a foothold in your psyche. The

Bible says, *Every day is a terrible day for a miserable person, but a cheerful heart has a continual feast.* (Prov. 15:15, GWT) Emotions are contagious, not only from one person to another but also from within. A smile on your face for having contributed to your world (in however minor a way) will reverberate in your body and in the body of the world.

# EXERCISES FOR PSYCHO-SPIRITUAL FITNESS

### THE WISDOM TO BE LEARNED FROM THE BIBLE

*God wants me to be joyful at work.*

### MEDITATIVE EXERCISE OF SELF-REVELATION

*Have I been patient, generous,
and good-natured toward my coworkers?*

### PRAYER EXERCISE OF GRATITUDE

*Dear God, thank You.
I am most grateful for everything.*

### INTENTIONAL EXERCISE OF SPIRITUAL REALIGNMENT

*I'll smile at work.*

## WORK IS EFFICIENCY; LIFE IS INEFFICIENCY

*Place ... confidence in God who richly provides us with everything to enjoy.*

1 Tim. 6:17 (GWT)

There is a story of a man who, exasperated by the slowness of a bus he was riding, asked the bus driver if he could go any faster. "Yes, sir, I can," replied the driver, "but I am not allowed to get off the bus."

You are entitled to be impatient with a slow-moving bus on the way to work but not on the way to visit friends, to a picnic, or on the way home. Try enjoying the view from this slow-moving bus, and if you do get off and walk, don't pass it. Rest is a very important balance for work and it is equally valuable in God's eyes. The Bible says, *Therefore, a time of rest and worship exists for God's people. Those who entered his place of rest also rested from their work as God did from his.* (Heb. 4:9–10, GWT) There is a mind-set for work (rigid time schedule, efficiency, goals to be reached) that differs from the mind-set of rest and leisure. You need to rest from your work, not only by not working but also by changing your mind-set about the efficient use of time and productivity.

In reality, time is not numerically structured; it is continuous and uninterruptible. In fact, there is no such a thing as time. Time is a mind-made concept. In nature, the rotation of the earth and moon around the sun generates a cycle of light and darkness and a spectrum of warmth and coldness. Time has a useful regulating function in society, as for example, when trains depart at certain specific times; but time's invasion into our mind is not in itself useful.

The mind creates tools, such as clocks and schedules, to regulate life and then becomes rewired by the tools it invented. The mind becomes its own victim. We all know people who always check the time. They are obsessed with being on time and extend their obsession onto others, getting as upset at someone for being late as they would if they themselves broke their obsessive schedule.

For some, time compliance is more important than its intended purpose, such as getting to work on time (but complaining about it) or coming home on time (but not enjoying it). The demands of "digital time" tax even the most obsessive minds—every minute must be accounted for. In short, the mind itself becomes a clock, always ticking.

At work, we are judged by our effectiveness and efficiency. Some people bring that modus operandi into their daily home life. Members of the family experience such persons as a boss or a school principal who insists on whipping them into greater productivity or efficiency.

- Write letters.
- Sing, whistle, or play musical instruments.
- Make things.
- Do all these things in slow motion.

Some view leisure activities as an inefficient use, if not a waste, of time. In fact, leisure time allows us to be with our families and friends or simply to be alone—inefficiently. Of course, we need to make special arrangements to be with friends at a certain hour and a certain place. But people who maintain an overly rigid schedule convert their lives into a constant state of performance and performing. They exist efficiently in each part of their compartmentalized lives, whether they are going to a party, fishing, eating, or making love. If they deviate from their organized existence, they become anxious. If others force the deviation upon them, they become resentful and angry. The clock determines their lives, as if they had to punch in for every activity. There is a time for eating, sleeping, showering, playing, reading newspapers, and so forth. Everything they do is structured and scheduled to the most minor detail and minute.

Outside the job situation, you need to get off the treadmill of schedule and enjoy your friends and family without the rigid structure of time. Living has less to do with doing than being. After work, get away from "musts," and "shoulds." Go to the "as is." Living is the opposite of productivity. It is freedom from any sort of categorical evaluation. Thinking and calculating deprive us of "the felt life." When you are home take off your watch. On weekends, there is no real reason to be so preoccupied with time (unless you might miss the last train home). If you are late to a four-o'clock movie, consider an alternative time or a different movie or even an alternative entertainment. The least desirable thing to do is hurry to get to the movie theater, yell at the people in your house to hurry, drive fast to "get there on time," and shout at drivers in front of you for slowing you down. The advantages of leisurely activities are quickly undone when time-related aggravation makes your body pump adrenaline into your system. Leisure time is to be lived in slow motion and savored languorously.

## CREATIVE ACTIVITIES BRING REGENERATIVE PLEASURES

*The Lord takes pleasure in his people.*

Ps. 149:4 (NKJV)

God takes pleasure in us. He takes pleasure in our pleasures and in our recreations and creative activities in life.

Recreational activities are part of our leisure time. If you convert recreational activities into work by setting up competitions, contests, and win-lose paradigms, they'll lose their "nonwork" quality. You'll be excited but not refueled. On the other hand, spontaneous playing for the sake of playing—gameful play—is as entertaining as it is refueling. You are not only entertained, amused, and unwound by these leisure activities but also socially engaged. You make friends through playing games, and through those playmates you find other entertaining activities. Some of these activities may help your physical fitness. You can take things in passively—by attending plays, shows, and book readings—or be a more active participant, as in playing golf, basketball or other physical games. At the end of either you are left excited or depleted, energized, or tired. You will have reacted physically and emotionally to what you have experienced. These activities reflect your interests, skills, competence, and physical and psychological fitness. But while the pleasure you obtain from such "outside" activities is fun, they are limited to a specific time and place and are always in need of repetition. They lack creative dimension.

Creative activities reflect your soul. These activities emanate from within and bring joy rather than fun. These activities are regenerative; they break free of time and space and are genuine reflections of your authentic self. For example, writing (in contrast to reading); playing an instrument, singing, or simply whistling (in contrast to listening to music); gardening (in contrast to going to a plant show); making furniture or knitting a sweater (in contrast to shopping); cooking (in contrast to ordering in). Everyone has the capacity for regenerative creativity. No matter how good (or not) you might be at any one of these creative activities, your soul will shine on them.

Leisure does not always mean doing something recreational or creative; it is also means doing nothing. You need to cultivate that art of pausing, the same way that pianists rest between notes. For that you need to rest and meditate in peaceful solitude. God says, *"Let's go to a place where we can be alone to rest for a while."* (Mark 6:31, GWT)

# EXERCISES FOR PSYCHO-SPIRITUAL FITNESS

### THE WISDOM TO BE LEARNED FROM THE BIBLE

*God wants me to enjoy life.*

### MEDITATIVE EXERCISE OF SELF-REVELATION

*Have I been enjoying my life?*

### PRAYER EXERCISE OF GRATITUDE

*Dear God, thank You for the things
You give me for my enjoyment.*

### INTENTIONAL EXERCISE OF SPIRITUAL REALIGNMENT

*I'll adjust my life to make room for creative
and recreative activities.*

*Scripture is the school of the Holy Spirit, in which, as nothing is omitted that is both necessary and useful to know, so nothing is taught but what is expedient to know.*

John Calvin, *Institutes of the Christian Religion, Book 3, 1539*

# CHAPTER IV

# STRIVING FOR GODLY STRENGTH

*Strengthen yourselves so that you
will live . . . doing what God
wants.*

1 Peter 4:2 (NCV)

When we say people are "strong," we usually mean they can withstand a great deal of stress. Such people are independent, self-reliant, can overcome adversity, never break down, and are unlikely to fail in their endeavors. These "strong people" have definite opinions, are confident of their judgments and actions, and are firm and practical. They possess a life philosophy of their own—a winning one. They are often intimidating, possess legendary anger, hold grudges, don't fear making enemies, and make their enemies' lives hell. When interacting with them, you'll almost always have to find a way to get along with these people, but don't expect them to try to get along with you. "He is the most commanding person I've ever met," a woman said admiringly about her "strong" husband. She continued, "He never apologizes because he is always right."

"Strong" people do what they want as long as it is within the boundaries of the law. A few test even those boundaries.

They aren't burdened excessively by guilt or remorse, nor are they necessarily interested in religion or concepts such as sin and redemption. They are tough and unforgiving of others and themselves. "Strong" people are seemingly near perfect and expect near perfection from everyone else. They are unsentimental and self-confident, and they never appear confused.

These traits may sound familiar and reasonable when one defines a strong person. But the Bible actually argues against each and every point cited above as a sign of strength.

## DON'T LET FAILURES GO TO YOUR HEAD

*Do not be surprised at the terrible trouble which now comes to test you.*

1 Peter 4:12 (NCV)

The Bible warns us: *In the world you will have tribulation.* (John 16:33, ESV) Yet God also comforts us with the encouraging statement, *"Do not be afraid."* This statement is found many times in the New Testament. No matter how committed you might be to your marriage, your job, your finances, your health, or to any other aspect of your life, you may fail. It may seem that the only way to prevent failure is to do nothing—don't marry, don't work, don't try. But there lies an even greater failure. You can safely anchor your ship in a harbor for a time, but ships aren't built to stay in port. Equally, you are not built to idle in a state of psychological inertia. Eventually, you must head to your destination, fully recognizing the risks involved.

When you fail at something, instead of despairing, welcome it as an opportunity to reinforce your faith. To get on the path to transformation you must get up on your feet after a fall, dust yourself off, and regain the power of the spirit. Do not let a failure contaminate your life with timidity and pessimism. Timidity and pessimism are spiritual prisons; don't let them paralyze you. The Bible says, *God did not give us a spirit of timidity, but a spirit of power.* (2 Tim. 1:7, NIV)

If you patiently carry on with optimism and forge your future (again and again), even if you fail at a specific task, you'll succeed at your larger mission: building spiritual character that transforms failures into successes. The Bible says, *Troubles produce patience. And patience produces character.* (Rom. 5:3–4, NCV)

"All sunshine makes a desert," goes a saying, and achieving success in life won't help you become deeply grounded. This can be illustrated by a bit of gardening knowledge. For example, bushes watered through irrigation have shallow roots that rest near the soil surface. These plants will die if the watering source they have become dependent upon malfunctions. Likewise, a steady stream of external rewards makes you vulnerable. Therefore, welcome (and smile at) occasional droughts. If you can tolerate temporary deprivations, they'll induce you to send your roots down deep and wide.

Often, failure darkens your mood, not because of the failure itself, but because of your reaction to it. Loss of a job, a demotion, a rejection by a lover, an illness or even getting old, all press the buttons of our insecurities. Being unwanted, unappreciated, and especially, unloved, is hurtful. But there are worse indignities in life: After a car accident left her quadriplegic, a twenty-eight-year-old actress decried the horror at having her once-beautiful body being cleaned by a rotating roster of caregivers. She sank slowly into the darkness of depression and rage. She prayed to die as quickly as possible. She begged the hospital staff to put her out of her misery. But one day her tirade against her body stopped. I walked into her room and found her smiling for the first time since the accident. She said, "my body is our body; caregivers' hands are my hands." I knew that the light had broken through her darkness. The Bible says, *The light shines through the darkness, and the darkness can never extinguish it.* (John 1:5, NLT)

- Smile at the indignities of life.
- Make a calling out of your misfortunes.
- Meet your pain with deeper faith.
- Be worthy of your suffering.

# EXERCISES FOR PSYCHO-SPIRITUAL FITNESS

### THE WISDOM LEARNED FROM THE BIBLE

*God wants me not to be discouraged by the tribulations of life.*

### MEDITATIVE EXERCISE OF SELF-REVELATION

*Have I been worthy in my suffering?*

### PRAYER EXERCISE OF GRATITUDE

*Dear God, thank You for helping me learn from my pain.*

### INTENTIONAL EXERCISE OF SPIRITUAL REALIGNMENT

*I'll not succumb to timidity and pessimism.*

## UNHOLY EMOTIONS WEAKEN YOUR SPIRIT

*Let us concentrate on the things which make for harmony,*
*and on the growth of one another's character.*

Rom. 14:19 (Ph)

The unholy emotions—anger, rage, hate—disturb the soul, damage the body, and harm relationships. This is why the Bible tells us: *Do not let the sun go down while you are still angry.* (Eph. 4:26, NIV) The brief satisfaction you derive from discharging these toxic feelings is surpassed by the fact that these emotions pollute you and everyone around you. When you feel but do not express negative emotions, they will still leak out and cause damage. Like remnants of toxic materials that are buried deep in craters, these emotions remain dangerous. And no one escapes the harmful effects. The Bible warns us: *An angry man stirs dissension, and a hot-tempered one commits many sins.* (Prov. 29:22, NIV)

However, toxic emotions, like nuclear materials, can be sources of energy if converted into a useful force. When you feel anger and hatred toward someone, take the following steps:

Face it. You are angry. Don't try to find a reason for it or explain it; don't look for a rationale and justification for it. Especially, don't seek revenge. That is God's privilege. The Bible says, *Do not take revenge, my friends, but leave room for God's wrath, for it is written: "It is mine to avenge; I will repay."* (Rom. 12:19, NIV)

Acknowledge that anger is an unholy feeling and contemplate God's Holy messages—love, care, and compassion. The Holy message is this: Love God and all his creatures, including the one who made you angry. The Bible praises the even-tempered: *Better a patient man than a warrior, a man who controls his temper than one who takes a city.* (Prov. 16:32, NIV)

Furthermore, if the goal of your anger is stopping someone's undesired behavior toward you, you'll be sorely disappointed. Negative emotions provoke similar reactions. The Bible says: *A patient man calms a quarrel.* (Prov. 15:18, NIV) It also warns, *A gentle response defuses anger, but a sharp tongue kindles a temper-fire.* (Prov. 15:1, MSG) Only love has transformative powers, and the holiest emotion—the love of God—is the ultimate transformer. "Love your enemies" means have no enemies. The universe is a hostile place for a pseudo-strong person but for the really strong person, a person strong in faith, it is a friendly place.

Thinking harshly of other people or talking critically about them only hurts you. The Bible tells us: *Whatever you have said in the dark will be heard in the daylight. Whatever you have whispered in private rooms will be shouted from the housetops.* (Luke 12:3, GWT) When you unleash feelings of hatred, envy, and anger they will directly or indirectly waste your own energy. The Bible urges us, *Let's agree to use all our energy in getting along.* (Rom. 14:19, MSG)

- Be calm.
- Don't stay angry.
- Don't gossip.
- Get along with other people.

In some dark corner of your psyche the heat of negativism may seem satisfying, but if you allow it to fester a little too long, it will burn you.

Negative thoughts and their corresponding emotions, deplete your psychic energy. You will be irritable and impatient in your interactions with others. In return, others will reciprocate your moods and reactions, further darkening your world. The Bible says, *You are only hurting yourself with your anger.* (Job 18:4, GNT) Negative thoughts and emotions (anxiety, anger, and depression) trigger damaging hormones and neurotransmitters (cortisol and adrenaline) that increase blood pressure and heart rate. For example, some neurotransmitters stimulate excessive acid production in the stomach and irritate the whole gastrointestinal system. Every cell in your body will suffer from the impact of these chronic traumas. In fact, victims of their own negative thoughts and emotions age prematurely and shorten their life spans.

Some people indulge in their anger as if it were an entitlement. Their expressions of hate become a source of power, and they use their negative emotions as allies against their enemies. They don't realize that negative emotions are enemies destroying from within. Get rid of negatives by walking away from them. Search for a positive view of a negative experience, or overwhelm negative emotions with positive ones, as if they were antidotes to a poison. Even better, vaccinate yourself against negative emotions—cultivate an all-loving attitude that preemptively dissipates all negative feelings. I have a nature-oriented version of this tactic that I've drawn from my modest gardening experience: plant more perennials if you want to get rid of weeds. The Bible says, *Fill your minds with those things that are good and that deserve praise: things that are true, noble, right, pure, lovely, and honorable.* (Phil. 4:8, GNT)

# HARBOR ONLY POSITIVE THOUGHTS

*Thoughts of peace and not of evil . . . give you a future and a hope.*

Jer. 29:11 (NKJV)

Life rarely is a smooth ride. The road of your life is punctuated with bumps, holes, and even craters. You also have wonderful moments in your life: sports victories, school shows, first loves, graduations, first jobs, marriages, births of children and their first days at school. However, it is those "bumps in the road" that remain most vivid in your memory. The memories of any sort of defeat—in school, in games, in love relationships, in business, in marriage—are always ready to surface.

Your mind is cluttered with thousands of thoughts, most of which are repetitive and circular. These thoughts range from wondering what "other people feel about me" to ruminating on "what life is all about." The more negative your thoughts, the more repetitive they become. Positive thoughts tend to be infrequent and fleeting. Being in good health, for instance, rarely registers as a positive thought and it definitely never becomes a repetitive thought. Similarly, you may experience generally positive thoughts briefly and move on to the negative, immediately adding some anxiety-, guilt-, or anger-producing qualifier: "Oh! She thinks well of me? Great, but why doesn't he?" "My life is wonderful. I am very happy. But how long will that last?"

The mind seeks the negative, either in the form of ruminating on the depressive past or conjecturing about the anxiety-generating future. The mind does not dwell on the present unless the present is depressing, anxiety-producing, or in some other way painful. While you can't escape the pain of now, you don't have to suffer the unchangeable past pain or unknown future pain.

Furthermore, don't scold yourself for having "bad" thoughts. To rid yourself of undesirable thoughts and feelings, repeat their opposing qualities, imprinting these in your mind again and again. For example, instead of chiding yourself for thinking, "I shouldn't hate him," encourage yourself by thinking, "I should love him." Keep repeating it until hate is replaced with love.

## A LITANY AGAINST YOUR PAST IS INNER POLLUTION

> One thing I do: Forgetting what is behind and straining toward what is ahead.
>
> Phil. 3:13 (NIV)

Some people rail unceasingly against someone in their past. Parents are often the targets of those who refuse to take charge of their present life. These people attribute their failures in adulthood to childhood experiences at the hands of "monstrous parents." It is true that some parents are malignant enough to inflict serious damage on their own children. Nevertheless, it's best to let go of a preoccupation with the past, especially when it is a negative past, because there are cumulative effects of active remembering. If you do not diffuse past negatives, your present associates—bosses, partners, teachers, spouses, friends—may become the convenient targets of your dissatisfaction.

Diatribes against people don't change who these people are. If these people are (or were) so bad, avoid them. You need to go to joyful places, events, and people, and recall only uplifting memories that enrich your soul.

"What if I have no joyful places, events, and people in my life?" you may ask. Well, that statement in itself is a form of a negative affirmation. Seek and you will find joyful places, events, and people. Begin by loving yourself because you're with yourself more than anyone else.

If someone said or did something to hurt you, tell him or her how painful the experience was for you. Give that person a chance to show remorse or even seek redemption. If he or she does not show remorse or request forgiveness, walk away. Don't think about how to retaliate in kind, which will only pollute your soul. *God doesn't want his children holding grudges,* the Bible says. (Phil. 4:2, MSG) A good example of cleansing yourself of ungodly emotions comes from nature: just as rain washes away dirt from leaves, bring down your spiritual rain to cleanse your soul when you confront an unholy encounter.

The story of Lot's wife turning into a pillar of salt as she looks back on the destroyed cities of Sodom and Gomorrah has been interpreted in various ways. In one version she was being punished for breaking her promise to God not to look back. In another version, her look back confirmed she was a participating member of the sinful cities, and thus she earned the same fate as the rest of the inhabitants. In still another version, her grief at losing her past was so great that the torrent of her tears covered her with salt. Looking back into the past (and I don't mean occasional glances but staring long and repeatedly) can leave you frozen in time. Reviling or longing for your past short-changes your present.

Past events and emotions are useful only if they serve the

"eternal now." This "now" is not a broken moment but a continuation of time. Extract knowledge from your past experiences, but don't dwell on the experiences themselves. If you ruminate obsessively about the past, it means you have not learned the lesson inherent in your experience. While visiting the past for a little time may help you recover knowledge, remaining there limits your present life. Free your emotions from the past and put your energy in the eternal present.

# EXERCISES FOR PSYCHO-SPIRITUAL FITNESS

### THE WISDOM LEARNED FROM THE BIBLE

*God wants me to be even-tempered.*

### MEDITATIVE EXERCISE
### OF SELF-REVELATION

*Have I been able to control my negativity?*

### PRAYER EXERCISE OF GRATITUDE

*Dear God, thank You for calming me.*

### INTENTIONAL EXERCISE
### OF SPIRITUAL REALIGNMENT

*I'll stop hurting others and myself
with my feelings.*

## LOSS OF FAITH IS THE ONLY REAL FAILURE

*If God is with us, why has all this happened to us?*

Jud. 6:13 (MSG)

Sometimes it seems helpful, at least temporarily, to project a failure onto external factors or to incriminate others in the failure. Being a victim of circumstances protects you from a harsher judgment: self-incrimination. For example, if you are injured in a hit-and-run car accident, you'll have a plain target for your anger and frustration. But suppose you injure yourself (or worse, hurt a loved one) in a car accident in which you're the driver? Your attempt to shift the blame to factors such as the other driver's lack of skill, a "slippery road," or "poor visibility," will go only so far.

Neither blaming others nor self-accusation will calm your soul for long. Your only salvation rests in believing that whatever happens is the will of God, and that it happens for a good reason, though that reason may not readily be apparent to you. Your role is simply to bear the pain. The pain that you endure without recrimination (either against others or yourself) will reveal your spiritual potential. There is no spiritual growth without tears.

You will become depressed and feel hopeless if you accuse yourself endlessly of causing your troubles. You will be angry and feel helplessness if you accuse others for your failure. You will be anxious and feel confused if you're intolerant of life's indignities. These are all temporary failures. But if these culminate in your losing your faith, then you'll be an eternal failure.

Loss of faith is an illness of the soul, and it is the ultimate failure. Loss of a job, friends, loved ones, health, and even your life are part of God's grand design. Hold on to what you love—your friends and family, your health, your life— but hold them loosely. If you do, then symptoms of depression, anger, confusion, and anxiety will not take you down when you lose what you have. However, if you hold your spirit loosely, you place yourself in danger of losing your ground. When you hold your life loosely and your spirit tightly, you'll never despair and your failures will be transfigured. Even discontent with the divine is pregnant with spiritual potential, provided you maintain your faith and smile at the indignities of life. It is written in the Bible: *We are hard pressed on every side, but not crushed; perplexed, but not in despair.* (2 Cor. 4:8, NIV) You will eventually accept suffering as a divine mystery.

If you lose your faith, you lose your self as well. This is not the time for improvisation, astrology, or psychology, all of which make us something less than we are. You've got to reset your compass quickly in a faithful direction. Faith will steady you. You may continue to wobble, but against the background of that faithful stillness. You may still have tough sailing for a while but you'll never get lost.

## MISFORTUNES SIGNAL THE NEED TO REALIGN YOUR SOUL

> . . . *I will turn their mourning into gladness.*
>
> Jer. 31:13 (NIV)

When good things happen, you rarely wonder about the source of your fortune. You may attribute your success to your intelligence, determination, hard work, and, occasionally, to luck. In fact, life's good fortune—with family, at work, in health, in creative activities—is the reflection of how well aligned your soul is with the Spirit.

- Don't complain.
- Don't blame.
- Don't argue.
- Don't accuse.

But when bad things happen, you search for the source of your misfortune. *"My God, my God, why . . . ?"* is the cry of every human being faced with suffering. You attribute your failure to your life circumstances and to your bad luck. Inevitably, you will make some changes in your circumstances. However, life's misfortunes are signs of a misaligned soul. Don't curse your bad luck or accuse others of bad faith; instead read your misfortune as a sign of the need to realign your soul with the Spirit. At times, such alignment occurs in an unexpected moment and by a quantum leap. At other times it happens through a steady and deliberate effort of prayer, contemplation, and discussion with your spiritual fellows. You can get wet in a torrent of rain or in a slow drizzle.

Direct spiritual failings—the commission of sinful acts—are obvious to everyone; however, indirect spiritual failings—the omission or absence of godly acts—often pass unrecognized because there always are extenuating elements that explain them away. Complaining, blaming, accusing, and arguing are the most common indirect manifestations of spiritual failure. The Bible says, *Do everything without complaining or arguing.* (Phil. 2:14, GWT)

Furthermore, it is useless to complain, argue, or blame,

for these activities rarely bring the desired results. A squeaky wheel may get oiled, but if it goes on squeaking it will get replaced. No one likes complainers and blamers, even when the complaints are justified. People tend to stay clear of complainers because they put the listeners into an awkward position: should the listener try to solve the problem or be quietly empathic? Should one comment if there are distortions or misunderstandings in the blamer's story, or even challenge the blamer's irrationality? A listener also may see him or herself as a future target of blame and try to avoid contact with the blamer. Eventually the blamers become isolated, and the isolation further impoverishes their souls.

Do your best at work or in a relationship; that is all that is expected of you. From then on you're in God's hands. If you must complain, complain to God. If you want to blame someone, you may blame God. He will not be offended nor will He withdraw His affection. "Why does God allow disasters to happen to me when He is supposed to love me?" you may ask. Well, God's love has different manifestations, which may, at times, take the form of disaster.

# EXERCISES FOR PSYCHO-SPIRITUAL FITNESS

### THE WISDOM LEARNED FROM THE BIBLE

*God promises to be close*
*when I am brokenhearted.*

### MEDITATIVE EXERCISE
### OF SELF-REVELATION

*Have I been allowing my spirit to be crushed?*

### PRAYER EXERCISE OF GRATITUDE

*Dear God, thank You for rescuing me.*

### INTENTIONAL EXERCISE
### OF SPIRITUAL REALIGNMENT

*I'll pick myself up and dust myself off*
*whenever I fail.*

# YOU CAN RESURRECT MEANING FROM YOUR SUFFERING

*But those who learn from their suffering,*
*God delivers from their suffering.*

Job 36:15 (MSG)

Everyone suffers at some time. Everyone loses a job, health, and loved ones. Some may be subjected to more suffering than others, but no one is immune. Misfortune varies in nature and intensity, but what determines the outcome is how you view that specific misfortune, and how *you* respond to the suffering.

If you view adversity as God's punishment, you may rebel against it or wallow in it. But if you view adversity as part of God's unknowable plan, you'll simply receive it. If you indulge in your suffering you will isolate yourself, and salvation is not found in disengagement. Meet your suffering with pure and deep devotion; you'll find Divine Solace. Transform the energy inherent in suffering into profound spiritual engagement and you will cease to hurt.

Life is defined by known or secret sorrows and sufferings. Each person tries to bear misfortune in his or her own way, sometimes stoically, at times less so. What makes suffering unbearable is being alone. Your loving relationships help buttress you against the sense of being alone in the face of trauma. Still, even though you feel their genuine, generous love and concern, sooner or later friends go home and family members naturally shift their focus onto their own tasks and preoccupations. The power of human relationships goes only so far, but in faith you are never alone. With God you will be able to face life's adversities with equanimity, regardless of how traumatic they might be.

In isolation there is self-pity ("Why me?"); hopelessness ("This is it, I'm finished."); sinfulness ("I should kill myself.") or worse sins ("I'll inflict my pain on others."). Misery may like company, but God considers inflicting pain on others an evil act. *I bore him in great pain!* Jabez's mother said in naming him (the name Jabez sounds like the Hebrew word meaning "he causes pain"). (1 Chron. 4:9, MSG) Later Jabez calls on God to change the meaning of his name to "he who does not cause pain." (1 Chron. 4:10, NKJV)

Negative reactions to pain and sorrow further isolate the sufferer. As the proverb goes, "You cannot prevent the birds of sorrow from flying over your head, but you can stop them from building nests in your hair." If you indulge in self-pity, hopelessness, and spiritual impoverishment, the proverbial birds will settle comfortably in your hair. Suffering is your reaction to pain and sorrow. Each of us is assigned to carry some of the weight of pain. Suffering stops when you understand, and gratefully accept, that the pain and sorrow you experience is a share of the burden in spiritual communion.

If you stay with your pain, in fact, if you allow it to cut deeper, you may find your purest tears of sorrow and your voice of longing. Meet your pain and transform it. Your soul is a prism for God's Divine Light. If your soul is faithful, it will transfigure your pain into sacred suffering. A serene peacefulness is embedded in sacred suffering much the same way that Divine Light is embedded in dark shadows.

STRIVING FOR GODLY STRENGTH

## SUFFERING IS A GOOD PLACE
## TO SEEK ENLIGHTENMENT

*I remember my affliction. . . . Yet . . . I have hope.*
Lam. 3:19, 21 (NIV)

It is human nature to avoid pain, and painless times are welcome gifts. Nevertheless, if extended too long and in too wide
an arena, that "no-suffer zone" tends to cushion people into
complacent superficiality. The agenda of people in the "no-
suffer zone" becomes that of how to maintain this bliss. Their
minds are preoccupied with the continuation of their physical
health, financial worth, and emotional satisfaction; they can't
enjoy what they have. Pain, illness, and loss can bring you
closer to seeing what you failed to see: the greater purpose of
your life. Use the physical symptoms and suffering of an illness as a sign to reorder your priorities. A spiritual response to
physical suffering—a folding into the loving and helpful
Spirit—can transmute suffering and pain to serenity.

- Don't rebel against your pain and sorrow.
- Don't indulge your pain and sorrow.
- Meet your suffering.
- Convert your suffering into a calling.

## YOU ARE STRONGEST AT YOUR BREAKING POINT

*The LORD is close to the brokenhearted; he rescues
those who are crushed in spirit.*

Ps. 34:18 (NLT)

No one is immune from being wounded in life. The question concerning suffering is not what to do *about* it, but

what to do *with* it. If you recognize the sacred nature of your wound and love it, God will rescue you. Regardless of the nature of your wound and the intensity of your pain and sorrow, your reverence will transform your wound into "the rose wound"—a gift from God.

- Be content with your vulnerabilities.
- Convert your weaknesses to gentle strength.
- Decode the message of your wound.
- Don't despair when you are at your breaking point.

If you don't recognize the sacred nature of your wound, it will scar eventually and you will miss the opportunity to receive the message hidden in your vulnerability. If you recognize the sacredness of your wound, it will be an opening to your soul. Though you will be inflicted with more pain as the wound widens to permit the Spirit to enter, and you will reach your breaking point, at that moment you will be healed, for healing is embedded in God's wound.

## PSYCHOLOGICAL VULNERABILITY IS A GENTLE STRENGTH

*When I am weak, I am strong.*

2 Cor. 12:10 (CEV)

We value and praise independence and self-reliance as signs of being grown up. But if you confuse maturity with seeing yourself as an entity separate from the world, you'll become alienated not only from your fellow beings, but also from God. The Bible describes the nature of strength as inner fortitude, not outer sources—such as power or wealth. By being independent of these transient gifts, you become dependent on the permanent source of power—God. *My power is strongest when you are weak.* (2 Cor. 12:9, GWT)

When you lose your ability to be vulnerable to others, everything you do becomes calculated. Even love and sex become items to be consumed rather than lived and shared. The invulnerable person can't be happy even in small ways.

Psychological invulnerability is a brutal strength. Zerubbabel, the governor of ancient Judea, asserts his power in the Bible: *"What are you, O great mountain? Before Zerubbabel you shall become a plain!"* (Zech. 4:7, ESV) Such "mountain levelers" are valued for their ability to cope with life's adversities, when, in fact, they fight hard to avoid being subjected to adversity. At times, these fights take ugly turns and they injure others, including loved ones, in the process of defending themselves. The mountain levelers often inflict serious harm on their victims for committing minor transgressions, although the stakes may not justify such harsh self-defense. For these people there is no higher authority than their own judgment. They see themselves as infallible in their choices and directions, whether these involve the selection of careers or friendships, which schools their children attend, where their children's marriages take place, or to which political party the family belongs. They may even claim to know more about religion than the clergy at their houses of worship. The invulnerable always see themselves as right and righteous, but as long as they perceive *themselves* as the source of their power, they remain alone and distant from God, and they are deprived of God's power.

Psychological vulnerability is a gentle strength. God wants you to say: *"I am glad to boast about my weaknesses."* (2

Cor. 12:9, NLT) If you gain gentle strength, there will be no adversities in life but multifaceted manifestations of love and mystery. Your soul is seen only through your vulnerability, and the depth of your vulnerability corresponds to the depth of your innocence, your trustworthiness, and your compassion for other beings. At this level of vulnerability, you are fortified with the strength of God.

## AT TIMES LET GO AND DEPEND ON GOD

*I know the plans that I have for you.*

Jer. 29:11 (GWT)

Daily life is filled with a steady stream of problems to be solved, obstacles to be overcome, and conflicts to be resolved. These issues may be as insignificant as traffic-related nuisances or as significant as finding a job or the right spouse.

You do your best to cope with these challenges, with varying degrees of success. Intelligence, determination, and judgment are sufficient resources for challenges that are man-made and even then, you can feel overwhelmed by the accumulation of minor negative events. Frantic recreational activities that are supposed to relieve your stress may only compound the problems. Whenever you feel overwhelmed, you need to retreat to your sanctuary, meditate on God, and feel safe and calm before you are able to relaunch into the world. God is your *querencia*—the place in the bullring to which a bull can safely retreat from the matadors—where you can pause and gather strength before returning to the fight. You must pause, however briefly, to regain the strength needed to battle the stresses of daily living.

Issues in life that aren't man-made, such as illness or natural disasters, are beyond the province of your intervention. Attempting to find solutions to such problems will generate a sense of impotence and helplessness and often will lead you to incorrect conclusions. Worrying depletes your inner resources and has no redeeming quality. It won't even motivate you. Even retreating into sanctuary and refueling yourself will not bring the solution that you seek relentlessly. This is when you turn the problem over to God and find strength in yielding. You need to give up the equation of "a problem, divided by recognition of it = a solution," and let yourself simply experience your dilemma, and have faith that God is not in a dilemma.

Make a habit of going to the sanctuary of God when you *don't* need His help. Such devotional practice helps you find sanctuary quickly when you really need it. In times of easy sailing, you may feel competent and in control of your life. You may feel that you don't need anyone's help—including God's. But when you hit a tempest, you'll realize how much you need God's guidance. Letting God take the helm is not passive resignation. You are actively bringing your mind to intertwine with the Divine Power. Don't go back and forth to God according to your needs. Stay with God. Let Him envelop your mind in all times, good or bad.

# EXERCISES FOR PSYCHO-SPIRITUAL FITNESS

### THE WISDOM LEARNED FROM THE BIBLE

*God wants me to feel strong when I am weak.*

### MEDITATIVE EXERCISE OF SELF-REVELATION

*Have I been complaining about my vulnerabilities?*

### PRAYER EXERCISE OF GRATITUDE

*Dear God, thank You for my weaknesses.*

### INTENTIONAL EXERCISE OF SPIRITUAL REALIGNMENT

*I accept my weaknesses, as they make me depend more on God.*

## BEING STRONG IS BEING GROWN-UP ENOUGH NOT TO SIN

*Stop thinking like children . . . in your thinking be adults.*

1 Cor. 14:20 (NIV)

So-called strong people are under the impression that they can sin and get away with it because they believe they are invulnerable, smart, and clever. They think they can justify or rationalize all their actions. In fact, this attitude is what eventually brings about the downfall of such a "strong" person.

- Don't violate Divine Laws.
- Cast your sins upon yourself.
- Fully compensate the harmed.
- Accept forgiveness as punishment.

A successful, middle-aged, married man tried to justify his affair with a married woman as harmless: "Look, we're not hurting anyone. Our respective marriages are sexually unsatisfying, so we both found a way to deal with our frustration. Our spouses have no knowledge of the affair. We don't flaunt it or push their noses into it. We are extremely cautious about being seen in public or doing anything to embarrass them. So where is the sin here? We do no injustice to our spouses; if anything our sexual liaison helps our marriages."

First, only the rightness of your will and whether or not it reflects the will of God renders justice. Second, sin is judged for itself, not by its effect. Last, life is lived by faith, not by intellect or reasoning. *The just shall live by faith,* says the Bible. (Heb. 10:38, KJV)

Sinful people pursue their will while negating His. Sin is transgressing God's laws. We don't need to be taught what sin is; the knowledge of sin manifests itself in the form of guilt. While the hereditary disposition to sin seems to be human, we also seem to be hard-wired to God at birth; we *know* His will. The battle between the disposition to sin and obedience to God is a chronic one. The Bible gives the best advice on how to avoid sin: *Turn away from the sinful things . . . Go after what is right.* (2 Tim 2:22, NLV) Sinning is the manifestation of a disobedient attitude toward God—a denial of the source of morality. There is no other standard of truth or norm of good.

Legal and ethical standards are external directions of law and society. They are civilizing structures for understanding right and wrong in your community. They represent expediency in punishment for those who act against those standards, if and when the transgressor is caught.

Morality is an internal direction of the Divine Will that proceeds from God and only from God. Morality provides a safe passage from immaturity to spiritual maturity. People who sin hurt others as well as themselves (though this may not be obvious). But punishment—guilt—is always included in the act of sin. There is no harsher punishment than self-punishment.

The Bible says, *For from within, out of a person's heart, come evil thoughts, sexual immorality, theft, murder, adultery, greed, wickedness, deceit, eagerness for lustful pleasure, envy, slander, pride and foolishness. All these vile things come from within.* (Mark 7:21–23, NLT) So does the only effective self-protection against them: the faithful conscience. Secular conscience operates with the rule of expediency. If you wonder whether you are right or wrong in any encounter, don't seek shelter in your mind. The mind is secular and will give you an answer, fit to your interest. The only wisdom you need is grace—the knowledge and the virtue accompanied and perfected by the love of God.

The Bible says, *The temptations that come into your life are no different from what others experience.* (1 Cor. 10:13, NLT) Equally, rewards or punishments are incorporated in all our deeds. The reward for the good deed—joy—isn't for the deed but is caused by the deed. Equally the punishments for sinning—guilt, remorse, and anxiety—aren't felt for the sin but are caused *by* the sin. Sin and its punishments are not isolated; they penetrate the sinner's core and bring a deep sense of alienation, for they exile the sinners from themselves.

You need only taste a drop of the sea to know that it is salty; so why do some people keep drinking seawater until they are salt-poisoned? It is for the same reason that sin leaves sinners eternally dissatisfied. Sinful people repeat their sins, hoping that the next one will bring fulfillment, but this repetition ultimately plunges sinners into an abyss of despair because a place empty of God cannot be filled. Every sin contains within itself a seed of destruction; sooner or later that seed will sprout and overwhelm whatever earthly gains are derived from the sin. The Bible describes the fate of chronic sinners: *Over and over God rescued them, but they never learned—until finally their sins destroyed them.* (Ps. 106:43, MSG)

Sinners are children disguised as adults. Their delayed spiritual growth allows them to succumb to temptation. They are not equipped to consider (or reconsider) the merit, fairness, or honesty of their intentions. They also are not equipped to consider (or reconsider) the danger, harm, and injury that are the consequences of acting on their intentions.

Because sinners' minds are like the minds of young children—responsible and irresponsible; rational and irrational; predictable and unpredictable; loving and hostile; calm and wrathful; selfish and altruistic—sinners need to be punished only by forgiveness. A compassionate response helps sinners to transcend infantile dualism. The Bible says, *God has . . . forgiven all our sins. (Col. 1:14, NLT)*

This transcendence is not necessarily a spiritual goal. It is being a grown-up and is a crystallization of your sense of self as a human adult. The Bible makes it simple: *When I was a child, . . . I thought like a child, I reasoned like a child. When I became a man, I put childish ways behind me.* (1 Cor. 13:11, NIV) Sinning is a childish thing. Spirituality must wait until a state of adulthood is attained. Your identity as a grown-up must be achieved and stabilized before you can use it as a base for spiritual growth.

Becoming is a slow and continuous process. Even after you grow up, leave your original family, and establish your own family, you are still in a state of psychological and spiritual formation. A youngster's physical and psychological maturation into adulthood is like the miracle that takes place in a vineyard where soil and water and sun nurture the vine to make grapes. An adult's spiritual maturation is like the process of fermentation in a winery, when grape juices distill to wine. Both psychological and spiritual transformations require the fertile environments of family and congregation.

Some people confuse adulthood and spiritual maturity with aging, and they fear of losing the joy, the zest, the energy, and the colorfulness of their lives. Maturity becomes associated with loss of desirability and loss of interest from others. The immature person is (supposedly) happy and the mature individual depressed. Nothing can be further than the truth. If anything, the immature tend to brood, be full of self-doubts, and insecure about everything concerning themselves, including their looks, intelligence, and worth.

Maturity is simply growing up and *God wants us to grow up.* (Eph. 4:15, MSG) In the spiritually grown-up years, we gain a lot: our mood is stable, and we are confident. Inner contentment shines over our daily lives. In mature years our sense of self crystallizes, giving weight and density to our character. Our experiences coalesce into a meaningful whole, giving us depth and vitality. In adulthood we stop experimenting with various life philosophies and firmly ground ourselves into a mature spiritual existence.

# EXERCISE FOR PSYCHO-SPIRITUAL FITNESS

### THE WISDOM LEARNED FROM THE BIBLE

*God wants me to grow up.*

### MEDITATIVE EXERCISE OF SELF-REVELATION

*Have I been a mature, responsible adult?*

### PRAYER EXERCISE OF GRATITUDE

*Dear God, thank You for succor.*

### INTENTIONAL EXERCISE OF SPIRITUAL REALIGNMENT

*I'll give up my childish, immature ways.*

## ACCEPT FORGIVENESS AND FORGIVE YOURSELF

*The heart is deceitful above all things and beyond cure.*

Jer. 17:9 (NIV)

The Bible tells us how incurably vulnerable we are to sinning. The issue becomes, then, what to do about it. First of all, sin can be your teacher if you are willing to learn. When you sin, you are lost but your sin can help you find your way once you recognize that your moral compass needs calibration. The purpose of sin is to bring sinners to a point of full transformation so that they no longer need to sin.

Ultimate serenity comes when you have nothing that requires forgiveness at the end of life. That is being strong. Your sin is designed to alert you to the need to alter your path and to be aware of your faults. You should not hide your sins, nor should you repeat them. Even the serious consequences of sins (being divorced, fired, or imprisoned) can help you if they lead you to seek salvation. The path from sin to grace is well paved. If you follow it, it will deliver you from your sins, restore your purity, and put heaven in your soul. The Bible says, *Live by the Spirit, and you will not gratify the desires of the sinful nature.* (Gal. 5:16, NIV)

Welcome the punishment of forgiveness. External punishment is a social and legal consequence of an unacceptable act. You may endure such external punishments; you may protest against them; you may be full of self-pity and plead for mercy; or you may feel that having paid the penalty, you may return to the same road (this time being a little more careful to avoid capture). Being declared "legally not guilty" carries no potential for redemption; if anything, it promotes further degeneration.

The door to redemption opens wide only if guilt is confessed, contrition and repentance (the hatred of sin, godly sorrow, and determination to live in virtue) extended, and the harmed compensated. The self-punishment that follows being forgiven is regenerative. The forgiven feel love and acceptance even if not legally exonerated and no longer feel compelled to repeat the transgression. Ultimately, what we all seek is to be loved and accepted for ourselves and to be forgiven for who we are—human beings.

There is a tendency to forgive others more easily than we forgive ourselves. In the abstract we clearly understand our fallibility, but when we fail we are shocked and dismayed.

To forgive another's mistakes is a generous and charitable act, but we are often not as charitable toward ourselves.

A source of such an ungenerous attitude is a lack of humility. You expect more of yourself than you do from others. Is this so because you are smarter, more competent, more knowledgeable, or better? "I am just a human being" is a humble beginning for self-forgiveness.

Another reason for the lack of self-charity is an absence of self-love. Forgiveness extended to others includes appreciating and loving them. Forgiveness is a gift that recognizes the value of the person who has made a mistake. Similarly, acknowledging yourself as "a good person, worthy of love and appreciation," may bring self-forgiveness. "But, I hate myself; I am not a good person, not worthy of anyone's love," is the cry of a lost soul. The only way to stop self-loathing is to love God. You'll quickly become a person worthy of love and appreciation in your own eyes.

## IMPERFECTION IS REAL AND POWERFUL

*Humble yourselves before the Lord, and he will lift you up.*

James 4:10 (NIV)

The quest for perfection is the enemy of good, for it leaves the seeker chronically dissatisfied. There is a difference between striving to reach your potential and yearning for some ill-defined level of perfection. Reaching your potential is possible; reaching perfection is not. There is no such thing as "perfect"; therefore, it is impossible to reach. Perfection is like the horizon: it gets farther away as you try to get closer to it. If you pursue either the horizon or perfection, you'll be on an unending journey. In trying to capture the nonexistent, you'll miss what you already have.

While the illusory seeking of perfection may exhaust and deplete the traveler, the self-delusional sense of having found it undoes all the good qualities in a person. Assumption of perfection, whether in the realm of physical beauty, intelligence, knowledge, psychological wellness—or worse, spirituality—makes a person feel, think, and act in a way that no one in contact with him or her can experience as genuine.

Then why seek perfection? Is it for the approval of God? But God doesn't seek perfection in humans. Is it to be loved by other humans? Although perfection (even as a concept) is admirable, it is not something others can relate to, never mind love. It is inauthentic. Is seeking perfection a defensive maneuver to hide human foibles? There is no shame or guilt in being human.

There is a story of a father who pointed to his paraplegic son and railed at God for his imperfect child. God's reply came: "Seek perfection in your reactions, not in your son's physical makeup." We are creations of God, imbued with all His mysteries and His intended imperfections. Therefore, accept yourself with all your imperfections and relate to everyone with the same awe and humility. Peculiarities are of God's making.

At least we often recognize the ill-defined nature of perfection and try to dismiss the quest for perfection. Unfortunately the same cannot be said for normality because, somehow, we all believe in the concept of being "normal."

To some extent what is normal is defined by culture, but it is always equated with sanity. We restrain our emotional life and creativity because we are afraid of being abnormal or being considered by others as such. In fact, striving to be "normal" generates most of our undesirable behaviors and unnecessary suffering. Professions that claim expertise in normality are unable to define what it is, but are very eager to identify certain thoughts, feelings, and behavior as abnormal, assigning diagnostic labels to them. If you inflict harm on others and deviate from the social norms, society will use its point of reference for the "standards of normality" and objectify your inner state.

- Don't seek to be "normal."
- It is okay to be confused.
- Don't fulfill your fears.
- Forgive yourself.

It is not unusual to suffer from things occurring in the external environment. But the soul should not suffer from within; these symptoms of self-torture must be heeded. If you inflict harm on yourself or suffer because of yourself, these symptoms are a sign that you need to make an adjustment in your spiritual life.

## CONFUSION THAT PRECEDES ENLIGHTENMENT IS STRENGTH

*You will receive power when the Holy Spirit comes on you.*

Acts 1:8 (NIV)

Only the spiritually enlightened are not confused. If you do not have faith, your moments of clarity are false, reflecting on self-satisfaction. Your conclusions will be no more than the clarity of self-congratulation. The confusion inherent in statements such as, "I don't know what to do with my life," or "I am not sure what life is all about," is much more valuable than the false certainty associated with the declaration of the sundry philosophies of self. Such certainties are false, though if repeated frequently enough they start sounding right and convincing. These mind-made pseudo-truths clutter the soul and leave no room for enlightenment. Unless you empty your mind of such false truths, light cannot penetrate.

While on the path to spiritual enlightenment you have to tolerate some confusion. This feels like being in a fog so heavy that you cannot see even a few feet in front of you. Forging ahead as if you could see far into the distance is the wrong thing to do. Those who deny they can't see and still move ahead miss the opportunity for spiritual gestation. Wherever they go, the fog moves with them. They may stumble onto gold and power or fall and destroy things (such as jobs, health, marriages, and other relationships). Worst of all, these people remain in a permanent fog bank, which they come to consider a natural state of existence. They get quite comfortable in the fog and the accidental introduction of light confuses them.

Real strength comes when you admit that only God knows. If you maintain your faith, you will be rewarded by the gradual lifting of the fog and will be bathed in light. Now, you can safely go in any direction; the light will follow.

# EXERCISES FOR PSYCHO-SPIRITUAL FITNESS

### THE WISDOM LEARNED FROM THE BIBLE

*God expects me to be just human.*

### MEDITATIVE EXERCISE
### OF SELF-REVELATION

*Have I been claiming false expectations?*

### PRAYER EXERCISE OF GRATITUDE

*Dear God, thank You for Your tolerance.*

### INTENTIONAL EXERCISE
### OF SPIRITUAL REALIGNMENT

*I'll patiently seek true enlightenment.*

*A little philosophy inclineth man's mind to atheism, but depth in philosophy bringeth men's minds about to religion.*

Francis Bacon, *Essays,* c. 1601

# CHAPTER V

# STRIVING FOR A GODLY MARRIAGE

*It is not good for the man to be alone.*

Gen. 2:18 (GWT)

It is not good for the woman to be alone either. Nor is marriage just a remedy for unhappiness. There is no path to happiness in marriage or in life in general. Happiness *is* the path, and by taking the path of happiness you will find a happy marriage.

## MARRIAGE IS A SPIRITUAL PARTNERSHIP

Marriage is a spiritual union in which two independent and equal individuals form a mutual interdependence. It is the subordination of "I" to "we," but not the loss of "I." Marriage is an organic union, a sealed blessing. In marriage, spouses deliver to each other reciprocal obligations: conjugal love, procreation, education of the little children of God, and prayer for a lifelong bond. The Bible says, *That is why a man will leave his father and mother and be united with his wife, and they will become one flesh.* (Gen. 2:24, NIV)

The ultimate purpose of marriage is not sex, security, companionship, or even love and procreation, though they all naturally fall under its umbrella. The primary purpose of marriage is the formation of a spiritual union with another person, and it is only within such a union that all other roles of marriage have meaning. Sex in a spiritual union is not just orgasm, but a personal manifestation of Oneness. Love in a spiritual union is not just an exalted feeling about someone; it is a personalized manifestation of our love of God.

When a man and a woman enter into the covenant of Holy Matrimony, their lives are blessed as a manifestation of the Divine. More than half of marriages fail because they are not grounded in the permanency of Divine Love. All reasons for marriage other than that of a spiritual union are transient and eventually dwindle away, leaving a large vacuum into which symptoms of dissatisfaction rush. Those who hope to find happiness in divorce and remarriage find an equally dissatisfying emptiness if the new relationship remains devoid of the spiritual passion drawn from the well of Holy Matrimony.

Holy Matrimony is a fertile medium in which to seek spiritual growth, both individually and jointly, for it provides unlimited opportunities for engagement, genuine caring, and deep affection. In Holy Marriage individuals learn to care about each other and the children of their union more than they care about themselves. Interestingly enough, such natural altruism is the best way of securing self-care, for those who are given to, reciprocate wholeheartedly and multifold.

- Foster union and separateness with your spouse simultaneously.
- Don't make the marriage the sole source of satisfaction.
- Be transparent to your spouse, but don't demand transparency.
- Expect and welcome crises and adversities.

Marriage is the most intimate relationship between two strangers and it is a natural ground for the cultivation of spirituality in tandem if both parties enter the marriage with the same awe as when entering a house of worship. The common reasons that some people get married—sexual passion, the need for security, the thing to do—provide neither lasting relationships nor lasting happiness. Passion especially is a feverish sedition of the mind against the spirit. As soon as the novelty wears off or passionate needs decline, the issues of living with someone and the conflicts emanating from spousal demands and failing expectations stir up ambivalence about each other and marriage itself.

However, if you accept the marriage as a spiritual partnership, it will last forever; even death won't keep you apart. There is no novelty that will wear off, no need that will decline. In a spiritual marriage, whether there is love at first sight or not, there will be love at all subsequent sights. As time goes by, spiritual marriage brings further density to a couple's love; in the last sight they confirm each other's everlasting faith.

# EXERCISES FOR PSYCHO-SPIRITUAL FITNESS

### THE WISDOM LEARNED FROM THE BIBLE

*God wants me to unite spiritually
with my spouse.*

### MEDITATIVE EXERCISE
### OF SELF-REVELATION

*Have I been fully committed to my spouse?*

### PRAYER EXERCISE OF GRATITUDE

*Dear God, thank You for
Your commitment to me.*

### INTENTIONAL EXERCISE
### OF SPIRITUAL REALIGNMENT

*I'll be totally committed to my spouse.*

## EVERY MARRIAGE NEEDS RETENDING

*Let your conversation be always full of grace.*

Col. 4:6 (NIV)

Marriage is a living organism; it needs be tended regularly and devotedly. Interactions between spouses are never predictable. Personal growth and change, individually and in combination, form a relationship that is a new and frequently confounding experience. A friend said to me, "I thought I knew myself, but since I got married I've discovered certain thoughts, emotions, and behaviors I never knew I had."

One dilemma you face in marriage is keeping yourself intact while entering into union with another person. This requires protecting your solitude and also protecting the solitude of your spouse. You can only be together by being two separate people and enjoying your own guilt-free solo activities. Marriage doesn't mean you must have the same friends, hobbies, habits, tastes, or preferences. Cultivate joint interests with your spouse but not necessarily at the expense of your own interest. For example, men often take more pleasure in sports than women do. If a husband wants to play golf or watch a football game on television, wives shouldn't sulk. Women tend to seek a social life. If a wife arranges dates with friends, a husband shouldn't be a reluctant partner.

Appreciate the "foolishness" of your spouse. Getting a manicure and pedicure or talking on the phone for hours is no more foolish than hitting a small white ball with a stick across a golf course or watching ten people running up and down a court trying to put a ball into a net. The soul needs to be indulged in pleasures, and what gives pleasure to one person may be totally uninteresting to another. For example, men are also social beings, but it is easier for them to socialize indirectly using a common medium, such as sports, business, and games. Women prefer direct and intimate conversation, and ridiculing these needs injures your partner's soul. In fact, aggressive challenges to such "peculiarities" may kill the soul of your partner.

Help your spouse, don't hinder him or her. God says, *"I'll make a helper suitable for him."* (Gen. 2:18, NIV) You were made by God to be suitable for and helpful to each other.

## ONLY SPIRITUAL LOVE CREATES TRUE INTIMACY

> *The fruit of the Spirit is love, joy, peace, longsuffering,*
> *kindness, goodness, faithfulness, gentleness, self-control.*
>
> Gal. 5:22–23 (NKJV)

Once they are married, people often feel the need to improve their spouse. That "need" is usually rationalized by saying it's for "your own good." And while there may be some truth in the concern, the benefit from your observation is usually undone by your criticism. There is one thing you can be sure of: whatever you reject as "imperfect" in your spouse will not be changed. If anything, your rejection will only perpetuate the perceived shortcomings. If there is a genuinely undesirable aspect of your loved one's behavior, your rejection must be directed to that specific matter, never generalized; you can identify or comment on self-destructive behavior in your spouse while accepting and loving him or her. There is no stronger incentive to change than being accepted by a loved one. If you keep criticizing your spouse, he or she will stop sharing inner thoughts and emotions with you. Pointing out someone's "imperfections" injures the soul, and the injured soul tends to hide its wounds. Your spouse will become a performer, an inauthentic person acting the role you've designated for him or her, in compliance with your demands. You will have won the battle for surface changes, but you will have lost your spouse on a deeper plane because an inauthentic person cannot relate to you in a genuine manner.

Women tend to judge men as inadequate in experiencing and expressing positive emotions and as trigger-happy in discharging negative emotions. Men tend to judge women as inadequate in contending with the serious business of life and as frivolous in pursuing interests. Whether these judgments have objective merit or not is not the issue. Judgment implies superiority. In soulfulness there is neither superior nor subordinate. When you judge your spouse you put him or her in a defensive position. Intimacy needs no explanation; just experiencing each other in depth is enough. Spiritual intimacy cannot flourish in a defensive atmosphere, which depletes and misdirects energy.

The soul is imperfect because we are always in the process of forming and evolving. The idea of perfection is an impossible goal. There is no one way of being, no constant normal. The only constants are differences. Soulfulness is appreciating the differences and enjoying your spouse's uniqueness. These bring color to life's drab "normality." The people who are controlled by their minds control their emotions; these people are rejected because they are neither hot nor cold. The scripture is graphic. *Because you are lukewarm . . . I will spit you out.* (Rev. 3:16, ESV)

# EXERCISES FOR PSYCHO-SPIRITUAL FITNESS

### THE WISDOM LEARNED FROM THE BIBLE

*God made me to be a helper to my spouse.*

### MEDITATIVE EXERCISE OF SELF-REVELATION

*Have I been respectful and protective of my spouse's individuality?*

### PRAYER EXERCISE OF GRATITUDE

*Dear God, thank You for accepting me as I am.*

### INTENTIONAL EXERCISE OF SPIRITUAL REALIGNMENT

*I'll cherish my spouse as he or she is.*

## BE TRUTHFUL BUT COMPASSIONATE

*Treat one another justly. . . . Be compassionate with each other.*

Zech. 7:9 (MSG)

Don't make a habit of drawing emotional blood from your spouse. Honesty without compassion is cruelty. Truthfulness should never override compassion, even though refraining from sharing the truth may require much effort on your part and consume a lot of energy. But if you live by your deepest values you'll never be depleted, for those values perpetually generate spiritual energy.

You can be as truthful to your partner as you are to yourself. Such revelation though, is accomplished with voluntary self-transparency, not by demand. Each person paces the depth of his or her self-disclosure. Transparency in a relationship doesn't come from stripping the other person bare; transparency is when you strip yourself bare. It is knowing and showing your strengths and your vulnerabilities, unmasking yourself, getting rid of layers of self-protective coats and defensive posturing and ridding yourself of the false self. Self-transparency is finding your own real essence; transparency is conveying that essence accurately to your partner. But don't expect your partner to respond to your baring your soul in the same way. This is not a command performance. Your transparency though, may enable your partner to experiment with (and then enjoy) sharing his or her self-transparency with you.

## THE SPIRITUAL MATE IS THE ULTIMATE SOUL MATE

*Because God created this organic union . . . , no one*
*should desecrate His art.*

Matt. 19:6 (MSG)

In my book *The Art of Serenity,* I discussed the nature of the soul mate and said that there is no stand-in for a soul mate and that finding and cultivating such strong emotional intimacy more than once in a lifetime is rare. This is true partly because it takes time to become soulful (obviously one cannot find a soul mate without being a soul mate) and it takes endurance to survive the bonding stages (the natural or induced crises and adversities) of soul-making. Union with the soul mate is a secular union, a highly personal arrival to which one aspires but at which one may or may not arrive. In the secular union a couple looks for and seeks grounding in each other. It is neither protected by an overarching celestial umbrella nor fertilized by a grounding soil. Such union, in a spiritual vacuum, is as extremely vulnerable as it is rare.

On the other hand, the spiritual mate is blessed from God above and tightly bound on this plane by your congregation. Spiritual love isn't about looking at each other; it is about looking together in the direction of God. Therefore, the profound connection of the spiritual mate is neither rare nor vulnerable. If you are single, embrace (almost randomly) someone in your congregation; he or she will evolve into your spiritual mate. Of course, you will make some personal choices and selections, but believing in God together is a solid base for effortless communion and for the ability to navigate all other variables. The spiritual mate is the ultimate soul mate.

## THE LOVE OF SPOUSE IS SEEKING SPIRITUAL LOVE

*Love . . . doesn't think about itself.*

1 Cor. 13:4-5 (NIV)

We commonly differentiate loving someone from falling in love—the passionate desire for someone. Passionate love is selfish love, though it hides behind the mask of self-sacrifice. The passionate lover strives to possess the beloved's body, soul, mind, and even past. This obsession to appropriate the lover, and the impossibility of it, is the source of uncontainable jealousy. The beloved can do nothing to reassure the passionate lover and dissipate the jealousy. Any act of assurance or promise of eternal commitment fuels the passionate lover's anxiety because such stands make obvious his or her separateness from the beloved. "I promise you." In that well-intended statement, the beloved articulates explicitly "I-ness" as being a distinct entity from "you." The passionate lover yearns to annihilate the beloved as a separate entity. This is the kind of fall that the Bible considers worthy of puzzlement.

> *There are three or four things I cannot understand:*
> *How eagles fly so high*
> *or snakes crawl on rocks,*
> *how ships sail the ocean*
> *or people fall in love.*

Prov. 30:18–19 (CEV)

Holy love is selfless, the most altruistic of all emotions. It carries no mask and hides nothing—it is what it is: pure love. Pure love is not possessive; it is not jealous; it is not devoted to the destruction of the beloved's self. Pure love protects the separate identities of people involved; it demands no reciprocation but gets it nevertheless; it demands no promises and offers none but remains steadfast nevertheless. It is in such perfected love that God abides: the Bible says, *If we love each other, God lives in us, and his love is perfected in us.* (1 John 4:12, GWT)

For the passionate lover, the beloved is just an object of love. Passionate love is the sinful treatment of another person as an object, a thing. Loving someone because of the person's recognized objective qualities is simply a reaction, a desire and an intention to take, in contrast to pure love. While the passionate lover targets certain external qualities, such as beauty, handsomeness, youthfulness, the holy lover sets no criteria; holy love can target anyone—beautiful or ugly, young or old, or physically challenged.

Once a passionate lover consummates the passion with the beloved, he or she tries to change the internal qualities of the beloved. The lover complains about the beloved's personality, choices of friends, hobbies, and interests, and way of thinking, feeling, and behaving. When the passionate lover asks the beloved, "Why can't you be like me?" he or she is seeking a psychological clone.

If you are the beloved, you may want to change, for there may be some truth in your lover's observations of you. But you can only truly change by accepting yourself. Holy Love accepts the other person as is, externally as well as internally. Holy Love, in fact, celebrates differences; it does not merely accept or tolerate them.

Passionate lovers never get to know each other because they are afraid of revealing themselves; they worry about being judged or may fear "being found out" and rejected. Consequently, they are in danger of "never being found" and missing the chance for genuine intimacy. Holy Love promotes self-revelation, including all imperfections, without self-scrutiny or self-censure. Such acceptance is the most fertile ground for growing spiritual intimacy.

## FAITH CREATES MIRACULOUS UNIONS

*What God has joined together, let man not separate.*

Matt. 19:6 (NIV)

The marriage of young people is a fertile ground in which they continue to cultivate their personal growth and to seed their marital union and future family. It is natural that at times married people feel overwhelmed and inadequate. It is important not to jump to the seemingly easy conclusions: "Maybe I am not suitable for marriage," or "Maybe this is not the right spouse for me." These questions are legitimate if made before the decision to get married, but if you feel you are not ready to be a spouse and are already married, leaving the marriage will hardly help you become a good spouse. Asking yourself whether you should be married after you've gotten married will only feed your natural ambivalence, leading toward divorce. Once God joins you, nothing should separate you from your spouse.

In fact, *none* of us is really *ready* to be a spouse or parent. We all have some healthy skepticism about our potential and tend to exaggerate our limitations when it comes to the marital union. But those doubts are natural ingredients of marriage; that is why marriage is considered a miracle. It was at a wedding ceremony in Cana that Jesus performed His first miracle: transforming water into wine. In marriage we transform doubts to certainty; ambivalence to commitment; discouragement to hopefulness; skepticism into total faith. Then you can become a fulfilled spouse and parent and gain blissful epiphanies. Faith creates miracles.

# EXERCISES FOR PSYCHO-SPIRITUAL FITNESS

### THE WISDOM LEARNED FROM THE BIBLE

*God wants me to seek love not in myself but in my spouse.*

### MEDITATIVE EXERCISE OF SELF-REVELATION

*Have I been conveying my love to my spouse?*

### PRAYER EXERCISE OF GRATITUDE

*Dear God, thank You for loving me unconditionally.*

### INTENTIONAL EXERCISE OF SPIRITUAL REALIGNMENT

*I'll love my spouse with all my soul.*

## DISCORD FEEDS THE SOULS OF THE SPIRITUAL COUPLE

*As iron sharpens iron, so one person sharpens the wits of another.*

Prov. 27:17 (GWT)

The Bible says, *Don't go to bed angry.* (Eph. 4:26, MSG) Nor should you get up angry. While occasional and reasonably justified quarrels feed the maturation of a couple, those who live with a steady dose of irritation, anger, scolding, threats, and retaliation may find unholy gratification in the conflict.

Sometimes couples either mutually lose their individual boundaries and become totally enmeshed with each other or one partner (usually the husband) takes the dominant role, if not the ownership of the other. Subsequently one spouse is treated as a possession, like a car, house, or a boat. The possessed usually becomes chronically unhappy and offers the only thing an object can offer—an impersonal relationship. The "owner" becomes the ultimate loser, totally missing the chance of finding a loving relationship and spiritual partner through genuine emotional intimacy.

Another pitfall in marriage—more frequently fallen into by women—is making the marriage the sole source of satisfaction, neglecting personal interests and friends. Interestingly enough, this behavior commonly is accepted by women's friends, as if their friendships are a holding pattern until one finds a man, because marriage is considered the ultimate goal. Even weddings are raised to such a high level of excitement that these occasions become not a means to an end, but an end in themselves. This can also happen if a couple has children. The woman who sees her sole role as that of devoted wife and mother and cultivates no outside interests is in danger of developing "gray fatigue," or numbness of the mind. She also is in danger of neglecting her relationships with her husband and the congregation and ultimately falling into spiritual impoverishment.

A family, no matter how spiritual it might be, is not immune from ordinary conflict. As long as ties among the family members remain intact and nourishing, there is no need for concern. If anything, benign neglect of garden-variety problems allows them to resolve themselves and strengthens the emotional resilience of those involved. The forceful attempt to tame those natural conflicts subdues the spirit of the family members. The dirt—envy, jealousy, selfishness, disrespect—must be *gently* washed from the family fabric. Excessive zeal in cleansing may remove dirt from the cloth but will also weaken its fibers. The same applies to the family structure. Excessive cleansing of problems harms the texture of the family. Adam was formed from mud and so are we. "Dirt" is best dealt with by the further cultivation of spirituality in the family.

Occasional disagreements and arguments with your spouse are not only inevitable but also desirable as long as the relationship is a spiritual one. Events may cause pain between you and your mate, and may even raise doubts about your marriage. You may forget your spouse's birthday or pay too much attention to an attractive stranger at a party; perhaps your spouse may be inattentive when you're ill. But don't indulge in hurtful moods and attitudes. The Bible says, *Don't grumble against each other.* (James 5:9, NIV) Couples who have not spiritually united gaze outward, accuse each other, and escalate the conflict. This culminates in one partner's angrily walking away from the other or retreating into cold silence.

THE SPIRIT OF HAPPINESS

Listen to each other's complaints carefully and gaze inward. Seek the truth within your spouse's complaint. You need not defend yourself; the validation of your spouse's perception of your wrongdoing—however insignificant it may be—is the first step toward transforming the conflict into soul feeding. "Yes, you are right, I did spend too much time with her at the party and not enough with you. I am sorry." Of course the issue does not end there. A number of questions may follow: "Do you find her interesting? Are you sexually attracted to her?" Each of these questions must be taken into the soul to resonate with truth. Answers must be honest but not injurious. Your spouse's sense of self as an interesting, attractive person can be protected when you avoid using comparative statements. Finding certain qualities attractive in someone other than your spouse is quite natural as long as you don't deny it and of course, don't act on it. If you share all that with your spouse, your souls will be touched and your spiritual union fertilized.

Jealousy is a natural emotion, provided that it serves in prompting more attention to your spouse. We are, at times, unaware of how wonderful our partners are. How many others could easily see virtues that we take for granted? And how many others are desperately seeking a spouse like yours? You tend to wake up if someone gets a little too interested in your spouse. That wake-up call, though, tends to be mixed with irritation, anger, and anxiety. Of course, if your spouse reciprocates the attention, no matter how innocently, all those mixed feelings could entrench and molder into corrosive accusations, rage, and even destructive vengefulness, all culminating in a vicious circle of mutual erosion of trust.

At the first hint of jealousy, stop and ask yourself the following questions: "Have I been spending enough time with my spouse? Have I been demonstrating my love and affection? Have I been sexually attentive? Have I expressed my appreciation explicitly and concretely?" The answers to these questions will guide you in your next step: attend to your spouse's needs. Most important, restrain negative emotions emerging from jealousy; be grateful, in fact, for the opportunity to take corrective measures. Jealousy is a signal that there is a need for the realignment of your relationship with your spouse.

Understanding the real purpose of marriage helps prevent disappointments or, worse, bitter struggles. Marriage is not the place to be rescued from yourself, to be taken care of, or in which to secure a sexual partner. It is neither a remedy for loneliness nor should it be used as a platform to enhance social and business standings. Although each marriage may have some elements of all of the above, marriage is all of those things and none of those things. It can neither be idealized as a solution to your life's dilemma nor reduced to a practicality of daily living. The idealized illusion of marriage by a vulnerable person is as dangerous as preventive disillusion of it by the cynic. Marriage is a holy union. Its purposes are to let you extend your love to your spouse and to encourage each other to expand the love of God, to give each other strength to serve Him, to create little human beings and to see them through lovingly, forming the next generation of God's servants. The Bible directs, *Encourage each other and give each other strength.* (1 Thess. 5:11, NCV)

# EXERCISES FOR PSYCHO-SPIRITUAL FITNESS

### THE WISDOM LEARNED FROM THE BIBLE

*God wants me not to remain angry
with my spouse.*

### MEDITATIVE EXERCISE
### OF SELF-REVELATION

*Have I been totally open and honest
with my spouse?*

### PRAYER EXERCISE OF GRATITUDE

*Dear God, thank You for Your encouragement.*

### INTENTIONAL EXERCISE
### OF SPIRITUAL REALIGNMENT

*I'll be attentive to my spouse's needs.*

## SEX IS A SPIRITUAL UNION

*Relish life with the spouse you love. . . . Each day is God's gift.*

Eccles. 9:9 (MSG)

Sex *without* spiritual engagement is bad sex, providing only bodily pleasures. It aims at orgasm; its physical power feeds the sense of the body and has no other purpose. It is an act isolated from the rest of life; therefore, it carries the potential of sexual and psychological aberrations. These aberrations may be benign, comical, tasteless, malignant, obscene, or dehumanizing. Frequently, vulgar forms are brought into this restless act by means of alcohol and recreational drugs, in an attempt to fill life's emptiness. Bad sex is depressing for it is futureless.

Sex *with* spiritual engagement is good sex. Couples who invoke the spirit in their sexual union create real families. Their hearts and souls are also organs of sex. Their physical and psychological engagement serve to draw each other to the depths of their abandon. Spiritual sex encompasses all the bodily sensations, including physical orgasm, but it is aimed essentially at the affirmation of values, love, and life. Its emotional power feeds the couple's souls and never offends their dignity. Good sex is not aberrant; it expresses genuine piety, the purest form of trust and innocence and chastity. This doesn't mean it need be flat sex without color and vivacity, an unromantic routine duty to be gotten over. Piety in sex means recognizing its fragility, taking it seriously, respecting the sacramental nature of the marital bed, and weaving the ritual of lovemaking into the larger purpose of life. Sex within God's law is free from any moral anxiety. Conjugal sex purifies, it sows seeds of love (literally) and is a path to spirituality through sensuous vitality. You should be playful and inventive without any embarrassment.

Good sex is the intimation of spiritual love when it is cultivated with erotic wit and intelligence and dignified passion. In the following lines of the *Song of Solomon,* a mortal is seeking the profoundest sexual trance in the intimation of the sublime love, where the mystical heights and depths are scaled.

> *Let him kiss me with the kisses of his mouth—*
> *for your love is more delightful than wine.*
> *Pleasing is the fragrance of your perfumes;*
> *Your name is like perfume poured out.*

Song of Sol. 1:1-3 (NIV)

Sex within the bond of lawful wedlock is to be enjoyed as much as it is to be reverenced. Sexuality isn't just an organic function of our bodies. The body is a sacred enclosure and opening it or entering into it requires love and respect. Good sex is a mutually offered, tenderly sought pleasure, culminating in giving of the body and soul. It ultimately brings us to the service of God through the desire for offspring.

In the animal kingdom the sole purpose of sex is procreation. We, of course, also procreate through sex, but have also discovered its many other uses—some innocent, some destructive or self-destructive. Every day we encounter destructive forms of sex in newspapers: a priest abusing youngsters; a relative sodomizing a child; a teacher impregnating a student. There are innumerable cases of rape, sadomasochistic behavior, pornography, and other deviant behavior, reported and unreported.

There are lesser-known forms of destructive sex that do not make the news. These are not reportable because they are not crimes in the legal sense of the word. For some, sex is a commodity to be stolen, for others an obsessive compulsion, for still others it is a boring chore. There is also a common misconception that passion ensues from transgression, justifying men's aggression toward women. These are crimes against the spirit, and they are often so subtle that the victim remains unrecognized.

## SEX IS A SPIRITUAL DANCE

*Why would you trade enduring intimacies . . .*
*for dalliance with a promiscuous stranger?*

Prov. 5:20 (MSG)

A sexual act is a manifestation of one's soul. The soulless person uses sex primarily, if not exclusively, to fulfill selfish needs. This person uses sex to discharge bodily tension and as an entertainment when bored, regardless of whether his/her spouse is interested. What makes sex a spiritual act is spontaneity and mutuality. Having an orgasm is a singular act. It is a lonely, one-person behavior. Good sex is a two-person behavior, a physical and spiritual embrace, a dance of two souls. It requires mutual desire and willingness. I am not talking about the much-praised simultaneous orgasm. The mutuality is not in time but in spirit—wanting to merge totally with your partner, body and soul, and experience oneness with each other.

Foreplay is not only what is described in sex manuals (though that is still better than launching yourself on your spouse). Sending flowers the day of the intended liaison and taking your spouse out for a fine dinner or entertainment are useful but they are just signals of interest. Spiritual foreplay is neither a signal nor a time-specific gesture. It is a way of relating to your partner. Spiritual foreplay is a loving presence in your spouse's life. When you reach such a state of relating to your spouse, you don't have to send any elaborate signals for your readiness; a quick glance, a light touch on the shoulder, a smile, a caress of the hair is sufficient. In fact, you may not even be conscious of sending such subtle messages. Furthermore, you'll be so simultaneously reciprocated that you won't be able to tell who initiated the love-making.

As for afterplay, there are no how-to books about this subject. Post-coital turning over to smoke or sleep is a common scenario for jokes. Spiritual afterplay is remaining in a physical embrace, talking about your love for each other, reaffirming your commitment to each other, and expressing your gratitude for God's gift: you love, you are loved, and you can make love.

When sexual intercourse is sandwiched between spiritual fore- and afterplay it is lovemaking, and it also is soul-making. But when sex is used for soulless purposes, such as fulfilling insecure neediness, expressing aggression, asserting dominance, easing boredom, reassuring virility, it only perpetuates these very same issues. Sex is not only a poor substitute for a solution to one's problems, but it also becomes contaminated by them. If you use sex for any reason other than spiritual union with your spouse, it will simply become intercourse. Whenever sex is used as a substitute, it compounds the original problem, and you will become addicted to sex in the same way that people are addicted to food, drugs, and alcohol. Such addiction is never satisfied by repetitive consumption, it is reinforced by it. Furthermore, when sex is contaminated by its use as a substitute, couples eventually develop sexual problems.

The common treatment of couples' sexual problems—reading sex manuals, watching sexually explicit shows, consulting sex experts who teach certain arousal techniques—goes only so far. Some therapists try to get couples to talk about their needs and to sensitize them to each other's needs. While some couples may benefit from sex education and training, talk therapy could actually exacerbate their problem. Talk, even between the best sexual partners—never mind the troubled ones—is the worst thing they can do. Too much awareness of either the body's or brain's activities interferes with natural acts. For example, walking is a voluntary muscular activity of the body, coordinated by automatic or autonomic semi-awareness of the brain. When you walk, the step ahead becomes the step behind. If you become conscious of this, you'll trip yourself. It is worse for the sex act because the organs involved function with involuntary muscles. Sex, like all other involuntary body activities, is interfered with by the intrusion of the mind. The mind reasons, justifies, explains, passes judgment, and can order the voluntary muscles to move but cannot give orders to the heart, the stomach, the lungs, the liver, and the sex organs. The harder you try, the less you'll succeed.

Once the phrase "Let's talk about our sex life" enters into the equation, whatever is left of your sex life will be gone. Sex does not include the thought of it or talk of it; it is the act—a felt reality. Sex is not an idea, a concept to be discussed and negotiated; it is to be experienced spontaneously. What-interfered-with-your-last-sexual-failure-and-how-to-prevent-it-in-the-future cognitive exercises only further inhibit you. Sex is not about the past or the future; it is about the "now," the immediate moment. Even asking your partner well-intentioned questions, such as, "Do you like my doing this?" "Do you prefer that?" "What do you want?" can inhibit the other partner. No matter how intimate you are with your spouse, you need not know all of his or her sexual mysteries. As the old saying goes, "Dissecting will only get you a lifeless carcass."

We make love the way we live our lives: some people are concerned only with their own pleasure; some are very sensitive to their partner's. Some people are reticent about sex; they experience it as frightening, intrusive, or engulfing. For others, sex is pure joy. The spiritually impoverished life most likely ends up with a spiritually dislocated relationship, including the sexual one.

We need to grow up spiritually to experience sex as a pure expression of love, joy, fun, and a potential or fruit-bearing union. And it isn't that difficult to get there. It requires only a small leap to satisfy one person's physical need to perform a loving act with another person. Above and beyond recognizing the partner's sensibilities, needs, and desires, you must recognize lovemaking as a gift from God to the two of you to enjoy together and only together. Lovemaking is a form of unwrapping God's gift with your partner, cherishing the moment and feeling cherished, experiencing real passion and the exaltation of blissful merging.

# EXERCISES FOR PSYCHO-SPIRITUAL FITNESS

### THE WISDOM LEARNED FROM THE BIBLE

*God wants me to enjoy sex
with my spiritual partner.*

### MEDITATIVE EXERCISE OF SELF-REVELATION

*Have I been providing joyful sex to my spouse?*

### PRAYER EXERCISE OF GRATITUDE

*Dear God, thank You for Your gift of sex.*

### INTENTIONAL EXERCISE OF SPIRITUAL REALIGNMENT

*I'll cherish this gift of God with my spouse.*

## RECIPROCAL FAITHFULNESS IS STRONG

*Live by the Spirit, and you will not gratify the desires*
*of the sinful nature.*

Gal. 5:16 (NIV)

Faithfulness is the one area in which you can demand full reciprocity from your spouse. If you have sexual intercourse with another person, you can no longer have a spiritual union with your spouse. He or she will become a person with whom you have sex.

Extramarital sex is another manifestation of the troubled soul. The soul enters an arena of destructiveness and self-destructiveness. The threat is not fear of scandal, concern about the disruption of the marriage, the threat to one's career or social standing; the worst punishment is automatically included in the sin of unfaithfulness: the loss of one's spiritual wholeness. Once you are unfaithful you can no longer be free and spontaneous with your spouse. Transparency is replaced with a deceitful façade, the psychic energy is directed to maintain lies and secrets, honesty is replaced with duplicity. This is one of the sharpest descents of the soul.

- Do not judge your spouse.
- Celebrate your differences.
- Offer only love for love.
- Forgive and forget transgressions.

A young money manager had a one-night affair while out of town on business. He couldn't explain bruises on his neck to his wife, except to confess the whole thing and ask for forgiveness. He told her "it didn't mean anything," that it was "just an impersonal skin-to-skin contact." He added that there was no relationship of any sort, he didn't remember the woman's name, and wouldn't even be able to identify her in a lineup. Maybe what he said was true. But to his wife the incident meant everything: it meant betrayal of the covenant, the violation of trust, and the contamination of their intimacy. On occasion people justify their sins in romantic exaltation. But the heights of affection cannot be reached in the descent to infidelity. The Bible says, *[The] unfaithful are trapped by evil desires.* (Prov. 11:6, NIV)

Recovery from betrayal is arduous and slow, and repairing the trust of your spouse and your family is difficult. You won't be believed easily. Not only will you be questioned about whether or not you are having sex with someone else; you also will be quizzed about everything else you do, including who you really are. Your spouse will wonder whether you are trustworthy, period.

When this occurs, a relationship not based on spiritual love tends to unravel. Such partners never sit down to try to hear the message in betrayal. "Are we in the wrong relationship?" "Have we outgrown each other?" "Have we neglected each other?" Should an act of unfaithfulness occur in your marriage, lovingly examine these questions together and do not only forgive the transgression but also forget it, as if it never happened. Forgetting is as important in life as remembering. The Bible says, *Forgive each other, just as God forgave you.* (Eph. 4:32, NCV). After your spouse expresses remorse with full consciousness and clarity and repents sincerely, resume your relationship with a clean slate, though your spirits will need some extra tending. Your faith will bind your wound.

When you obey God, you will always be faithful, effortlessly. You won't be blind to seeing lovely, beautiful, smart people; you won't be deaf to hearing the tempting whispers. The Bible recognizes that *you want to do what's right, but you're weak.* (Matt. 26:41, CEV) But you'll become more determined and recommitted to your marriage with each temptation. Because *God . . . will not let you be tempted beyond what you can bear. But when you are tempted, he will also provide a way out.* (1 Cor. 10:13, NIV)

# EXERCISES FOR PSYCHO-SPIRITUAL FITNESS

### THE WISDOM LEARNED FROM THE BIBLE

*God wants me to forgive my spouse
for causing me pain.*

### MEDITATIVE EXERCISE
### OF SELF-REVELATION

*Have I been unforgiving of my spouse?*

### PRAYER EXERCISE OF GRATITUDE.

*Dear God, thank You for forgiving me.*

### INTENTIONAL EXERCISE
### OF SPIRITUAL REALIGNMENT

*I'll forgive and forget my spouse's transgressions.*

*When the Doctrine of the Gospel becomes the Reason of our Mind, it will become the Principle of our Life.*

Benjamin Whichcote, *Morals and Religious Aphorisms*, 1753

## CHAPTER VI

# STRIVING FOR A GODLY FAMILY

*Children are an inheritance from
the Lord.*

Ps. 127:3 (GWT)

The ultimate purpose of sex is procreation—to beget the next generation—and the ultimate reason for marriage is raising those spiritual children. Having a family means being responsible for others. At a basic level it means being a reliable provider. God looks harshly upon those who fail in this fundamental role. The Bible declares that failing to provide for the family is a failure in faith, and adds, *If anyone does not provide for his relatives and especially for his immediate family, he has denied the faith and is worse than an unbeliever.* (1 Tim. 5:8, NIV)

## CHILDREN ARE SPIRITUAL SOULS IN FORMATION

Raising children has several dimensions: physical, psychological, and spiritual. Although the physical needs of children may seem to be overwhelming, especially in the early years, these are rather simple, fairly straightforward, and uncomplicated—food, clothing, shelter, medical care, schooling—when compared with spiritual needs. Children are entrusted to us especially to ensure they receive spiritual abundance.

You have children to love them just as you were created from immense love of God and branded with His seal of acceptance and worthiness. You must unfailingly convey the same messages of acceptance and worthiness to your children and continue to do so until the day of their own revelation of God.

Every child is a sign of hope: An old life is confirmed; a new life is secured, and eternal life is reassured. If, at an early age, children are taught they are the immortal children of God, their characters will be shaped with strength, hope, confidence, and optimism. You'll be joyful in knowing that their belief of living forever in eternal blessedness contributes to their honesty and gratefulness. This belief is voiced in the Bible: *I have no greater joy than to hear that my children are walking in the truth.* (3 John 1:4, NIV)

God gave life to His children, and our job is to give our children to God. Unchecked by the spirit, instinct and intellect may lead to moral decay. As a parent, you hope your offspring will be honest, caring, studious, hardworking, and productively engaged in social and communal life. In most children the problems associated with "developmental arrest" are actually the result of undiagnosed "spiritual arrest."

During adolescence children don't verbally declare their atheism, but they act out their lack of faith. They may become involved with the wrong people, drink, take drugs, get into trouble with the law, and engage prematurely in sexual activities. There are hundreds of books, talk shows, and expert opinions that deal with raising physically and psychologically healthy children and preventing children from getting lost in undesirable and dangerous patterns of behavior. Obviously, we have not yet found the answer; otherwise we would see the end of these how-to books and professional advisers. Some experts come close to being helpful when they say "love your children." But parental love, however necessary, is not sufficient. In fact, children's negative behavior quite often slowly erodes parental love. The children's negative behavior moves parents from unconditional love to "tough love"—so that parents are forced to set rigid rules.

There is a single solution to your concerns about ensuring desirable outcomes and preventing undesirable ones: instill the love of God in your children at the earliest possible age. Until the age of six or seven, children cannot conceptualize the abstract idea of God, so when they make God a concrete form, they are not engaging in a type of idolatry. Let them grow up a little and then nudge them toward the mature idea of God.

Educating children about God requires tolerating their need to locate Him by using their five senses and their own criteria of existence: "Why can't I see God?" "Why can't I hear His voice?" "How old is God?" "Is God a boy or a girl?" "Where does God live?" "Who are God's parents?" "How does God speak?" The subject of God has the potential for teaching the children not only faith, but also how to grow out of concrete thinking. The following are one parent's answers to his child's questions: "God is visible by His creations; silence is His voice; God is ageless; God is both a boy and a girl; God lives everywhere; God's parents are love and goodness; God speaks in the Bible." His answers are a good example of how to handle a young child's questions in an age-appropriate way while encouraging the child to continue asking "why" questions.

A friend of mine told me his four-year-old daughter asked her mother whether God looked like a little girl. The child was expanding on her mother's earlier statement that "she was created in God's image." My friend confessed that for a moment the woman was at a loss in the face of her little girl's intelligent question. Finally, the child's mother said, "Yes, God is good and you are a bundle of goodness." Of course, there is always the safe and appropriate answer: "I don't know."

In language appropriate to your children's ages, inculcate them with the desire to imitate God's love: first, within the nuclear family (parents, siblings); then within the extended family (grandparents, uncles, aunts, cousins); then with neighbors, friends, teachers, and ministers; and ultimately expanding outward to other people as well as animals and nature.

- Make your home safe and comforting for your children.
- Give each child a full measure of love.
- Do your best to be a good provider.
- Always remember that your children are entrusted to you by God.

Children, of course, adopt this loving attitude by identifying with their loving parents. But the family that relies solely on human love will find it hard to maintain such a loving attitude under adverse circumstances. If, however, you teach your children about God's love for them and the rest of the world, they will love all of God's creations as they'll recognize and cherish their kinship with them.

The love of God is the source from which all other love

springs. Children who are instilled with the love of God do not cause their parents to worry about them. These children hold the promise of turning out to be good people and they are protected from destructive and self-destructive forces. God's children are protected equally from undue fears and anxiety. My friend's four-year-old girl worried that the moon might fall down on their house. Despite her mother's reassurances that the sky is like a roof holding the moon in place, the child wasn't comforted until she was told that God wouldn't allow the moon to fall and that she should look forward to its nightly visits because the moon is a friend of God.

# EXERCISES FOR PSYCHO-SPIRITUAL FITNESS

**THE WISDOM LEARNED FROM THE BIBLE**

*God wants me to be a good physical
and spiritual provider.*

**MEDITATIVE EXERCISE OF SELF-REVELATION**

*Is my highest priority allocating my resources
toward the needs of my children?*

**PRAYER EXERCISE OF GRATITUDE**

*Dear God, thank You for providing for me.*

**INTENTIONAL EXERCISE
OF SPIRITUAL REALIGNMENT**

*I'll focus on providing for my children
to the best of my ability.*

# IMPRINT FAITH IN CHILDREN DURING THEIR VERY YOUNG YEARS

*And all thy children shall be taught of the Lord.*

Isa. 54:13 (KJV)

You keep your infants warm, protected, and well-fed. You love them, kiss them, hug them, and sing them lullabies. But you also need to embrace them with faith and, when they get a little older, cultivate spiritual literacy. Children are hardwired for God, but they still need to be programmed to process the teachings of God. It is no different from training them in civil behavior; children are innately good but they still need to be taught the rules of civility.

In addition to physically giving birth to children, mothers play a primary role in psychologically birthing them. The role of the father in the early years is widely dependent on his disposition. Some fathers are fully involved when their children are born; others wait a year or two before they become fully engaged.

- Make home your children's spiritual kindergarten.
- Imprint them with the love of God.
- Do your best to provide spiritual abundance.
- Live a devotional life, don't just tell of it.

Fathers play a significant role in "civilizing" children; that is, setting limits, laying down rules, teaching laws of reciprocity, and establishing conditions for love. This isn't to say that mothers love their children unconditionally, but they come close to it. Nevertheless, mothers' attachment to their children, though essential for the survival of their youngsters, eventually requires some tempering. Fathers are helpful in that process; their entrance into the mother-child unit helps mother and child separate.

But both parents weigh equally when it comes to meeting the spiritual needs of children. If you and your spouse aren't equally committed to a spiritual life, your children will become confused. If one of you is a nonbeliever, the doubts cast on faith may undermine your child's emerging spirit. Children have inquisitive natures and are easily seduced by the labyrinths of the mind. They place their belief in the power of reason and derail themselves from the path of faith. We have to inculcate children with faith. A five-year-old girl was told by her pregnant mother that God had answered their prayers and was sending a little brother for her. The girl, disconcerted, replied that *she* hadn't prayed for God to send a little brother. "But," said her mother, "you do pray without asking for anything don't you?" The girl nodded, and her mother continued, "You see, God knew what you should have." The child was convinced though not pleased.

There need be no such extraordinary moment or event to teach children about God and faith. There is no specific time or place to educate children about the words of God. Simply start doing so at the earliest age possible and on every occasion. The Bible says, *Fix these words of mine in your hearts and minds. . . . Teach them to your children, talking about them when you sit at home and when you walk along the road, when you lie down and when you get up.* (Deut. 11:18–19, NIV)

Children learn by two different methods: imprinting and conditioning. Imprinted learning is through osmosis—

taking in the environment. Imprinting is effortless learning and it occurs before age six or seven. The way we learn to speak our first language, for example, is through imprinting. Information that is imprinted in the brain is as solidly ingrained as genetic material. That is why children introduced to faith before age six are effortless believers. After the age of seven the ability to imprint begins to decline. From then on children must learn through conditioning, which requires enormous conscious effort. In contrast to imprinted learning, learning by conditioning is never stable.

At birth, uncontaminated by the mind, we are bundles of emotions, including joy. For the previous nine months we inhabited the most secure place imaginable. We were warm and fed on a steady stream of digested nutrients. We did not even have to breathe or go to the bathroom. The primary sound we heard was the comforting, regular, and rhythmic pulsation of predictability: our mother's heartbeat. When we are pushed out of our paradise—not an easy voyage—we emerge into a strange world. People with enormous faces make deafening noises. It is cold—at best it's 72 degrees in the delivery room, 26 degrees below the temperature we were accustomed to—it is much too bright, and there are no boundaries. If our mouths aren't quickly buried in our mothers' breasts, overwhelming anxiety, if not panic, ensues.

The anxiety of the unknown, unpredictable, and boundless is true not only for the first day of our lives, but also for the rest of our lives. Children are especially in need of a secure, reliable, reassuring, and comforting home. And there is no security and comfort anywhere better than having a spiritual home. Children are conceived with the blueprint of Spirit. It is your job to help them to build their own spiritual home. You do that by bringing your children to God. The Bible says, *Train a child in the way he should go, and when he is old he'll not turn from it.* (Prov. 22:6, NIV)

## BRING YOUR CHILDREN TO GOD

> *Do not let any unwholesome talk come out of your mouths,*
> *but only what is helpful for building others up according*
> *to their needs.*
>
> Eph. 4:29 (NIV)

You teach your children to walk by encouraging, cajoling, and holding their hands; so too, must you coach them to walk to God. But most important, you teach by example: let them see you walking the walk. Faith cannot be taught without living it. Your children learn effortlessly by imitating, absorbing, and identifying with their parents' behavior and language. All they need is exposure to your words and deeds and to trust your sincerity. To hear the notes in a melody, you must sing it. If you don't really believe in God, but you think the idea of God is a good thing for your offspring to know about, you'll only hinder their innate belief in God. At best they will quickly adopt your intention and behave as if they believe in God. The Bible says, *Let the little children come to me, and do not hinder them.* (Luke 18:16, NIV)

It is only through emotional, visceral knowledge of God that children become believers. For this they require a genuinely spiritual home, in addition to the teaching of concepts of the sacred, prayer, and worship, which children cognitively learn.

Some people think that it is fair and just to allow children to choose their religion. On the surface this seems a way of empowering children, but deep down it generates enormous anxiety for them. To make choices is always unsettling, regardless of the importance of the matter. We are ambivalent creatures; even choices as insignificant as what to order in a restaurant or what to wear to work can make us uncomfortable. Choices with escalating significance, such as which school to attend, where to live, and whom to marry, frequently throw us off, bringing us to the impasse of indecisiveness.

Imagine children having the power to choose their religion. That type of freedom is not a privilege; it is a sort of punishment. The whole posture of allowing this choice is a misunderstanding of human nature. Our quest to belong is also our cry for restraint from the "freedom" of having to make choices about our most important source of existence: our spiritual communion. Your children need you to formulate a guiding idea for their existence. God is not a matter of choice. The Bible says, *Train a child in the way he should go.* (Prov. 22:6, NIV) Unless the salvation of restraint is imposed upon us at a tender age, we will never know the way and we will never know the security of spiritual communion.

# EXERCISES FOR PSYCHO-SPIRITUAL FITNESS

### THE WISDOM LEARNED FROM THE BIBLE

*God wants me to bring my children to Him.*

### MEDITATIVE EXERCISE OF SELF–REVELATION

*Have I established a spiritual home
for my children?*

### PRAYER EXERCISE OF GRATITUDE

*Dear God, thank You for entrusting Your
children to me.*

### INTENTIONAL EXERCISE
### OF SPIRITUAL REALIGNMENT

*I'll talk patiently of God to my children and
enthusiastically show them my devotional life.*

## MEET YOUR CHILDREN'S EXCESSIVE DEMANDS WITH GODLY PATIENCE

*Love is patient.*

1 Cor. 13:4 (GWT)

As infants we are at one with our mothers; we consider our mothers an extension of ourselves and expect them to understand what we want them to do without our uttering a word. We respond with frustration, impatience, and incredulity to our mothers' inability to understand the nature of our demands. Not delivering what we want sparks rage.

Children cannot differentiate their requests from themselves. Refusal of requests becomes tantamount to negation. Mothers are equally aware that children's infantile narcissism needs gentle tempering if the children are to outgrow it. Parents are able to recognize children's "unreasonableness," and "making a mountain out of a molehill," and innately decipher the underlying demand. Sometimes parents choose not to deliver.

Mothers' intentional failing promotes children's separateness. No matter how painful that separation may be, it is absolutely essential that it occur before prekindergarten to prepare children for peer relations. Furthermore, understanding children's demands and choosing not to deliver (whenever it is appropriate) is even more useful to children's growth then satisfying their demands. Such "failings" help transform their childhood narcissism into healthy self-love, provided the children are simultaneously reassured of their acceptance by their parents.

Ongoing provision for and denial of children's demands

helps them learn that not all demands are acceptable and that rejection, whenever it occurs, is specific to the demand and is not to be generalized to other, appropriate demands. The denial of demands should definitely not be associated with rejection of the children. At times children's demands may not be understood and responded to, but the children are always accepted and loved. The spiritually enlightened mother conveys that message without much effort. She doesn't think, "I should reject the request but accept the child." She just does it. For her, this is not a technique or a behavioral teaching game. It is real. In compliance with God's wish she fails, and in failing she gives her children the tools that will help them mature.

Infinite patience produces better-than-expected results. Children learn to separate and individuate through questioning and quarreling with your answers in the form of self-assertions. Parents have to cultivate godly patience if they want to be helpful. A scientist was asked, "Which teacher was most responsible for your success?" He replied that it was his uneducated father. Every night at the dinner table his father asked the same thing: "Son, what good question did you ask today in class?" The scientist went on to explain, "There were two messages in his question: One, that he had the confidence in my ability to ask questions. Two, that I'd ask only good questions." You can be immensely helpful if you can convey to your children that it is not only okay, but desirable for them to ask questions and that every question they ask is a good question, even if they question your authority.

Assertions of young children are geared toward gaining autonomy through self-mastery. An enlightened attitude toward them is that of godlike patience. As long as there is no danger to their well-being (children cannot be allowed to light a fire or run a bath), there is no reason to get into a struggle with them. They are simply trying to be self-sufficient. In fact, their practice of independent functioning has nothing to do with you, until you enter the picture to interfere with their agenda. "We are going to be late to Grandma's," yelled the parent to his young child, who was trying to put on his shoes and tie his shoelaces. The exasperated parent forced the child's feet into his shoes, hastily tying the laces. The child had to be carried out to the car, crying. A more enlightened parent would have preferred to have been a few minutes late to an event and explain the tardiness to whoever required an apology, rather than preempt the child's burgeoning self-mastery.

Seeds of adulthood, independence, and self-confidence are sown in the early childhood years. Occasionally you may meet people who are very confident but not particularly intelligent, experienced, or educated. You wonder how on earth they acquired such self-possessed, if not spiritual, composure. Well, the answer is in those green years they were allowed, if not encouraged, to tie their shoelaces by parents with godly love, patience, and encouragement.

## MEET YOUR ADOLESCENT'S EXCESSIVE SELF-ASSERTION WITH GODLY TOLERANCE

*Whoever receives little forgiveness loves very little.*

Luke 7:47 (GWT)

There is a story of a wise old man who was challenged by a young prankster. The townsfolk were gathered around the wise man, listening to his advice, when a young man stepped up, holding a small bird tightly in his hand. He asked the old man if he could tell if the bird was dead or alive. The young man was going to prove the old man wrong regardless of the answer. If the old man said, "The bird is alive," the young man would crush it; if the old man said, "The bird is dead," the youngster would let the bird fly away. The old man looked into the young man's eyes and said: "It is up to you, son; it is up to you."

Adolescents separate and mature by the aggressive rejection of authority. Even though your adolescent's behavior may challenge your capacity to forgive, you must. Otherwise, your child will never learn the nature of real love, and his transient, phase-related, undesirable attitude will be entrenched into adulthood. This is a difficult phase for both parents and adolescents. The assertion of childhood is replaced with aggression. You, as a parent, are the obvious target for an adolescent's aggression but if you squelch it others will be targeted: siblings, other family members, teachers, school officials, and police officers. Adolescent negativity is quantitatively and qualitatively very different from that of younger children. Occasionally, the demand for autonomy, coupled with the rejection of parents, is hard to take. This is the time to be the most spiritual. At times you may have to walk with heaviness, saying, "Fine."

- Don't retaliate against children's aggression.
- Don't reciprocate children's sexuality.
- Disapprove of children's behavior but not of them.
- Be patiently loving whenever you are tested.

Adolescents define themselves by opposition. You have to learn not to be upset about it and never to retaliate with rejection. One parent said to a sixteen-year-old daughter: "Look, if you dislike us so much why don't you just leave?" That sort of naked confrontation is not useful. If repeated, the youngster either will take you up on the offer or, worse, stop fighting with you. Like salmon, adolescents swim against the stream. Unlike salmon, adolescents spiritually die not at the end of their mission, but if interrupted, during the trip. Uninterrupted, adolescent struggles end in the calmer waters of young adulthood, where they spawn goals and ideals and begin to define themselves, not by being against something but by being *for* something.

God wants us to empathize with adolescents struggling to become adults. We need not see ourselves as challenged by opposing youngsters but as working together in the spiritual continuum of ages, albeit in separate phases of life. It is not "us versus them," but it is "us in different stages of spiritual sameness." In that sense, it is up to us, the adults. How? Being secure in the face of our adolescents' self-assertions and conceding power to them by delegating responsibility to them for themselves. It is not about feeling challenged by the adolescent, but being able to take a risk and say, "It is up to you, son (daughter); it is up to you."

## CHILDREN'S FAMILY ROMANCE MUST BE MET WITH GODLY JOY

*May the God of hope fill you with all joy.*

Rom. 15:13 (NIV)

Young children identify with the same-sex parent and compete with the opposite-sex parent (and wouldn't be unhappy to lose the competition in play). This is not a worn-out Freudian Oedipus complex: boy loves mother and kills father in fantasy. In real life this is a God-given joyful passage.

During their first year and a half, both boys and girls prefer to be with their mothers. They tolerate the father, finding him especially tolerable if he has certain maternal traits or assumes some maternal duties. Otherwise, the father is just an intruder into the safe haven of the mother-child dyadic matrix. Children don't need anyone besides the mother, and they definitely don't want a man who competes with them for their mother's time and attention. In return, a father may feel neglected by his wife and resent her; he may become irritated by the children clinging to his wife and feel alienated in the household. A father scolded his two young children and his wife with too-obvious self-pity: "What am I here for? Just to make money, so that you three can play house? I work all day, come home and get a peck on the cheek, and then I'm totally ignored for the rest of the evening." Later that night he accused his wife of avoiding sex with him under the guise of putting their youngster to sleep by lying down in the child's bed and staying there until he [the husband] fell asleep. His wife's protestation was that if she didn't lie down with the child, he would come to their bed, making the situation worse. Frequently, she confessed, she fell asleep even before their son did.

A spiritual father would smile at observing a youngster's attempts to have an exclusive relationship with the mother. Fathers: do not triangulate—don't see the situation as "me, her, kids." Know it as "us." Do not feel excluded, though for a while you may be a little on the periphery. Husbands: be delighted that your wife and children are in such a close-knit relationship, even if it seems to be at your expense. Only jealousy can make you think that others' relationships are made at the expense of yourself. A wife's giving priority to children is natural and desirable. It would be a matter for concern if a woman remained fully attentive to her husband at the expense of their children.

In the preteen years, when the need for their mother's exclusivity is long ended, children commonly position themselves closer to the same-sex parent and begin to distance themselves from the other. This is the age of identification with the same-sex parent. A nine-year-old boy likes to play ball with Dad, ride in the car with him, chat with him, wear his clothes, imitate his walk and speech, and always talk about him to friends. At this age boys simply are proud of their fathers. On the other hand, boys begin to be embarrassed by their relationship with their mothers. They don't like to be hugged or kissed, especially in front of their friends. They don't even like to be picked up from school by their mothers. Mothers tend to understand their sons' behavior and know that no matter what, in the privacy of the home, boys will reverse their attitude and get close to them. Under stress, even the most macho boys metaphorically run to hide under their mothers' skirts.

Preteen girls are tougher on their fathers. For a father to get a little peck from a preteen girl is a major event. Unlike boys' reactions to their mothers, girls aren't embarrassed by their fathers' affection; rather, it is an innate reaction of keeping a desired, but unacceptable, male at bay. The more fathers request, plead or attempt to kiss their preteen daughters, the more they will flee: "Oh, Daddy, leave me alone." The only possible way a father can attain any emotional closeness to a preteen girl is by not pursuing. The best strategy for dealing with preteen reticence is to follow the "pigeon theory." If you go after pigeons—even with grain in your hand—they'll run away, but if you sit still they'll come and eat out of your hand . . . eventually.

Occasionally, a preteen child manifests sexual interest in a parent. It is usually so obvious that everyone in the family is quite aware of it and it even becomes the subject of jokes. But the child would be deeply hurt and offended by the parent's slight or the family's mockery.

The preteen child's sexual interest in the parent is not exactly "sexual." The child doesn't mean to have sex or even share a passionate kiss; the child just wants to be desired. To be desired as a sexual object is quite different from being loved as a child. To be desired is a precursor of adult sexuality, where nonsexual affection is replaced with sexual aggression. You have to allow yourself to be a transitionally targeted desire for your children; it is a rehearsal for their future sexual and other relationships. Your role at this stage is to be a recipient of their desire and to see your children through a healthy passage into maturity.

God wants you to be hopeful about the outcome of your spiritually raised children and *not* to be too bothered by their phase-specific behavior. God fills us with hope. You need to see time as a continuum. "Now" is a fleeting moment, to be experienced, savored and—at times—suffered, but never despaired of, because "now" serves as the platform upon which to build tomorrows. Children's "now" behavior is exactly what it should be. Your "now" sentiments—hurt, rejection, anger—must be felt but not be indulged. You are witnessing the passage of time in your children. Not too long ago, you were there yourself: you are experiencing another manifestation of eternal recycling.

# EXERCISES FOR PSYCHO-SPIRITUAL FITNESS

### THE WISDOM LEARNED FROM THE BIBLE

*God wants me to impart joy to my children.*

### MEDITATIVE EXERCISE OF SELF-REVELATION

*Have I been wholesome in my interactions with my children?*

### PRAYER EXERCISE OF GRATITUDE

*Dear God, thank You for Your infinite patience with me.*

### INTENTIONAL EXERCISE OF SPIRITUAL REALIGNMENT

*I'll be lovingly patient with my children.*

THE SPIRIT OF HAPPINESS

## DISAPPROVE OF THEIR BEHAVIOR; DON'T DISAPPROVE OF THE CHILDREN

*By believing you receive God's approval.*

Rom. 10:10 (GWT)

Frequently, I hear parents trying to tame their children's un-desirable behavior with some form of generalization: "Why are you so unpleasant?" "You are always fighting." "You are too selfish." "Why can't you be like your sister?" Exasperated at her fourteen-year-old son's stubbornness about everything, including eating, smoking, neglecting school work, and stay-ing out past curfew, a mother cried out, "I just don't know what to do anymore." A child psychologist suggested family therapy, which the boy rejected. When forced to go to ses-sions, the child sat and never said a word. The family's min-ister advised the mother to be lovingly wise and devise a way to extricate herself from the power struggle with her son. The mother pitifully confessed that she had neither the wis-dom nor the love left to do so. She failed to see the potential in her child instead of his actions. It is at such desperate times that you should seek sanctuary in God. The Bible says, *If any of you lacks wisdom, he should ask God.* (James 1:5, NIV)

Parental godliness is possessing the ability to approve of your children without their deserving it. This means if you identify a pattern of behavior in your children as unaccept-able, don't generalize it to an all-encompassing disapproval of them. God's unmerited favor is bestowed upon every child. While disapproval of a behavior may condition chil-dren to change, disapproval of the child reinforces perpetua-tion of the undesirable behavior. Children read disapproval as being unloved and will repeat bad behavior again and again to test—in fact to verify—that they are unloved. Then there is no turning back. Such children will expand their bad-behavior portfolio to the point that they bring about their own greatest fear: confirmation of being unloved.

To save sibling relationships, as well as your relationship with your children, differentiate children's attitudes, behaviors, thoughts, and feelings from the children themselves. A young girl pointed at her brother and accused: "You are a liar!" When the mother disapproved of her language, the child provided evidence of her brother's lying. "Mom, he swore he didn't take my atlas; I found it here, under his mattress." The boy stood by, sheepishly and ineffectively trying to find an explanation. The mother turned to the girl and said, "No, my dear, your brother is not a liar; he lied." Then the woman turned to her son: "Any attempt on your part to explain how her atlas got under your mattress would be another lie." The girl wasn't persuaded. "What's the difference? He lied, so he is a liar." The mother explained: "Someone who lied can stop lying, right?"

Even better, instead of saying to a child "You lied" or "You did a bad thing," you might say, "What you have done isn't worthy of you." While limiting the criticism to the specific act, in contrast to generalizing ("you lied" versus "you are a liar"), protects children from developing a negative sense of themselves; higher expectations promote self-esteem and make perpetuation of the undesirable behavior less likely.

Children lie because their souls are just beginning to take shape. During the formation process, the child's soul makes up stories to fill holes in it. When the soul is totally formed there'll be no room for lies. Similarly, children's raw aggression and sexuality reflect their souls in formation. Once formed, their souls will be tamed and will appropriately direct them to serve God in truth.

Fights among children may be provoked by as minor an event as one taking the other's toys, pencils, or candies. They may scream, yell, even hit each other, and demand your arbitration—each on his or her side, of course. If you are just and kind, even if you disapprove of a specific behavior, both sides will walk away a little unhappy. But they will, at some level, recognize your fairness and not feel discriminated against or unloved. On the way to forced peaceful coexistence, children may utter such statements as "I hate you!" and "I wish you were dead!" to each other. Nonetheless, soon they'll forget what the fight was all about and resume playing with each other. However, if you disapprove of the children, not just their behavior toward their siblings, they will actually grow to hate each other. Children cannot hate you—they need you—and they will displace all their negative feelings on your other children, especially on the child they perceive as your "favorite."

God tells us never to use unwholesome language when disapproving of children's behavior. *"Do not let any unwholesome talk come out of your mouths."* (Eph. 4:29, NIV) "Bullshit, what did you do with the money?" said a father to his son, who claimed that he had lost his weekly allowance. If the father intended to find out if his son was lying, he didn't succeed. He succeeded only in putting his son on the defensiveness, teaching him nothing. If he had said, "Son, be always sure that whatever you do is worthy of you," he might have seeded a hope for the future. Here, the covenant of respectful and spiritual communication was broken. Both father and (probably) son did things that were unworthy of them.

Home is a school in which to teach children to be spiritual beings. Your children shouldn't see their siblings as rivals for your love. Love is simply there; it's not given to one at the expense of the other. Lovability carries no conditions. Love is not a prize for good behavior. Likeability, on the other hand, is conditional. There is likeable and unlikeable behavior. It is expected that unlikeable behavior is changeable. The change, though, primarily occurs through inner forces. If you teach children to understand God through and through, they'll change. It is in the Bible: *Fix your attention on God. You'll be changed from the inside.* (Rom. 12:2, MSG)

An eight-year-old boy named Simon was very impatient with his five-year-old brother, Matthew. He treated Matthew roughly and refused to play with him. Simon made no concessions in his stand against his brother, no matter how hard his parents pleaded with him to do so. Then Simon's parents stumbled onto a line in the Bible: *You shall be called by a new name, which the mouth of the Lord will name.* (Isa. 62:2, NKJV) This was a blessing in anticipation of change. Simon's parents sat with him, read him the line, and asked him if he were to be renamed what name would he prefer to have. Simon replied: "Rock." "We hope you will be worthy of your name," his parents said.

The following day Rock not only played with his brother, but also took him to play with other older boys. When they came back from the ball game Rock had a beautiful smile on his face. He said, "See, I am different." He could not have known the story of Isaiah: *See, I am doing a new thing!* (Isa. 43:19, NIV) God must have touched him.

# EXERCISES FOR PSYCHO-SPIRITUAL FITNESS

### THE WISDOM LEARNED FROM THE BIBLE

*God wants me to approve of my children.*

### MEDITATIVE EXERCISE OF SELF-REVELATION

*Have I been approving toward my children?*

### PRAYER EXERCISE OF GRATITUDE

*Dear God, thank You for approving of me without my deserving it.*

### INTENTIONAL EXERCISE OF SPIRITUAL REALIGNMENT

*I'll praise my children even when I disapprove of their behavior.*

*What are all the gifts of the Gospel; are they not all mental
gifts. . . . And are not the gifts of the Spirit everything to man?*
William Blake, *Jerusalem,* 1820

# CHAPTER VII

# STRIVING FOR GODLY FRIENDSHIPS

*You are better off to have a friend*
*than to be all alone . . . if you fall,*
*your friend can help you up. But if*
*you fall without having a friend*
*nearby, you are really in trouble.*

Eccles. 4:9–10 (CEV)

## FRIENDS ARE OUR ALTERNATE SELVES

Friends are spiritual fellows in faith and spiritual brothers and sisters. All sins and virtues flow from a common well. We suffer and rejoice together. Enlightenment makes us alike, endowing believers with homogeneous values and wisdom; enlightenment also regulates the past, present, and future. We inhabit the same earth with our friends during our lives and when we die we inherit the same earth as our friends.

We know our fellows and they know us. See the holiness in friends and demonstrate the intention of intimacy with them by words, including how you address them. The Bible says, *Greet each of our friends by name.* (3 John 1:15, GWT)

Humans are always in formation. Your state of being is not whole unless you are being for others. In others you nurture your faith, and find yourself.

# EXERCISES FOR PSYCHO-SPIRITUAL FITNESS

### THE WISDOM LEARNED FROM THE BIBLE

*God wants me to have friends.*

### MEDITATIVE EXERCISE OF SELF-REVELATION

*Have I been cultivating friendships?*

### PRAYER EXERCISE OF GRATITUDE

*Dear God, thank You for being my friend.*

### INTENTIONAL EXERCISE OF SPIRITUAL REALIGNMENT

*I'll be a good friend.*

## FRIENDSHIP REQUIRES SELF-TRANSPARENCY

*Each of you must put off falsehood and speak truthfully.*

Eph. 4:25 (NIV)

Being transparent to others allows them to experience your joys and sorrows. Similarly, when others are transparent to you, you'll resonate with their emotional life. Your fellows' successes will uplift your soul. Their defeats will break your heart. Sing in life with them; weep for them in death. King David lamented after the death of his friend Jonathan: *"I am heartbroken over you, my brother Jonathan!"* (2 Sam. 1:26, GWT) In fact, the death of a friend is like a mini-death for us, not unlike the death of a sibling.

You need friends with whom you can openly and honestly share your thoughts, feelings, and urges, even when these are unacceptable. You need, without fearing rejection, humiliation, and degradation, to be totally transparent with friends. You want your friends to recognize your potential for spiritual derailment and you must allow them to help you back onto the road of safety and purpose. Spiritual friendship is, of course, mutual. You must be available to your fellows and help them to reveal the darkest corners of their souls. Receive them with love and compassion and offer them the path toward salvation.

- Be transparent with your friends.
- Suffer your friends' pains.
- Delight in your friends' joys.
- Confess your sins to each other.

Genuine friendship is precious, for it is a spiritual kinship. Once found, it needs to be carefully guarded, nourished, and celebrated. Friends, as our alternate selves, bring us their joys and happiness in life, and their pain and suffering too. Some people run from the pain and suffering of their friends, as if those feelings are contagious diseases. They want only fun in friendship. "I have my own problems," one person told me, "I don't need the problems of my friends. I want to get together with them to get away from my issues, not to be swamped with theirs." That is not real friendship.

It's true that emotions are psychologically infectious. In the presence of someone sad we might feel down; in interacting with the joyful we might feel elated. That is exactly the point: God wants us to feel sad with a sad friend, happy and joyful with a happy friend. You cannot run from your pain, nor should you run away from the pain of friends. Their pain is your pain. The Bible calls it *fellowship of suffering*. (Phil. 3:10; Heb. 10:33–34, NIV) Sharing the pain with friends alleviates some of the burden. Although the pain remains, the intensity of suffering subsides because what makes pain and suffering unbearable is enduring it alone. Spiritual friendship is a powerful antidote to being alone. Never negate your friend, especially at his darkest moments, even if he negates God. The Bible says, *A despairing man should have the devotion of his friends, even though he forsakes the fear of the Almighty.* (Job 6:14, NIV)

What defines a spiritual friendship is its inviolate principle: nothing is wanted, needed or desired, except love and affection based on God's love. Spiritual friends are gentle in nature but straightforward in stance. They are our alternative consciences. The Bible says, *Confess your sins to each other and pray for each other so that you can live together whole and healed.* (James 5:16, MSG) Instead of holding your lapse captive in the dark tribunal of self-judgment, offer it up to your spiritual fellows. They can shed light upon the unknown and unknowable. Confessing to them will lead you back to innocence by their forcing you to take responsibility for your wrongdoing. They will provide a compassionate external tribunal and will end the torture of your inner tribunal. In the company of your spiritual fellows you will find that your virtue will flourish. The Bible urges, *Encourage one another daily . . . so that none of you may be hardened by sin's deceitfulness.* (Heb. 3:13, NIV)

# EXERCISES FOR PSYCHO-SPIRITUAL FITNESS

### THE WISDOM LEARNED FROM THE BIBLE

*God wants me to share with my friends
all joys and sufferings.*

### MEDITATIVE EXERCISE OF SELF-REVELATION

*Have I allowed myself to share my joys and pains
with friends, and have I been receptive to theirs?*

### PRAYER EXERCISE OF GRATITUDE

*Dear God, thank You for Your offerings of joy
and suffering.*

### INTENTIONAL EXERCISE
### OF SPIRITUAL REALIGNMENT

*I'll be transparent with my friends.*

## FRIENDS ARE OUR ALTERNATE FAMILY

*A true friend sticks by you like family.*

Prov. 18:24 (MSG)

Unfortunately even our most intimate friendships tend to lose importance after one of the friends marries. Once people marry, they relegate friendships from their lives as single people to a somewhat dispensable position. Although married partners cultivate new relationships with others (usually couples and often parents of their children's schoolmates), they tend not to maintain close contact with old friends, especially if those friends remain single. Years, perhaps decades later, married partners nostalgically remember and even attempt to reestablish contact with long-forgotten companions, who often yearn equally for the past relationship. But once reconciled, these former friends find very little to talk about except old memories. Long-interrupted relationships are difficult to resurrect.

Friendship is where we begin to separate from our families. Separation from mother during the "terrible two's" is a dress rehearsal for the psychological birth of the child. Emotionally connecting to a peer outside the family is the *actual performance.* At every age friends define who we are, who we are not, and the nature of our struggles. They also define the issues, fears, and wishes that we experience together. Friends are life-witnesses to our becoming. Friends see themselves in each other. Nonspiritual friends are transitional relationships; they are more appropriately called acquaintances and are traded as circumstance dictates, such as change of job, change of town, joining or leaving a club or an organization. Spiritual friends are friends for life, if you treat them as holy connections.

- Stay in close contact with your friends.
- Don't trade away your friends for marriage.
- Be humble with your friends.
- Praise virtues of your friends.

Some families discourage their children from developing strong friendships because they fear losing their children to strangers. I overheard a parent saying to an adult daughter, "Friends come, friends go. Only family stays." In reality, without friendships, even family ties lose strength. Lack of friendship isolates and impoverishes the soul, which, in turn, weakens all other relationships, including family relationships.

Spiritual fellowship is a gift from God. It is a love relationship, not with the friend himself but with the friend's virtue. It is a mutual effort to bind each other's souls to God. When you find a virtuous person walking toward you, run to him or her. The trust between spiritual fellows has roots in the implicit recognition that God witnesses these encounters and offers His encompassing embrace. You must embrace your spiritual fellows equally, regardless of their accomplishments, power, or position in life. Never take into consideration someone's hierarchical standing in society. Humbly approach your spiritual fellows with an open heart and even some self-subordinating acceptance. This is why the Bible tells us: *Clothe yourselves with humility toward one another.* (1 Peter 5:5, NIV)

# EXERCISES FOR PSYCHO-SPIRITUAL FITNESS

## THE WISDOM LEARNED FROM THE BIBLE

*God wants me to be humble with my friends.*

## MEDITATIVE EXERCISE OF SELF-REVELATION

*Have I been showing humility toward my friends?*

## PRAYER EXERCISE OF GRATITUDE

*Dear God, thank You for humbling me.*

## INTENTIONAL EXERCISE OF SPIRITUAL REALIGNMENT

*I'll embrace my friends with utmost openness and modesty.*

## SELECT YOUR SPIRITUAL FELLOWS
## FROM YOUR CONGREGATION

*I choose as my friends everyone who worships you
and follows your teachings.*

Ps. 119:63 (CEV)

There are few rules limiting your selection of spiritual fellows: obviously they cannot be family members. Your spiritual fellows are best chosen from your own congregation, people with whom you may feel a special affinity. In choosing friends, observe them talk, laugh, and listen. You may even test them by sharing some minor confession and then seeing what they do. Do they get upset and scared or run away? Do they understand, gently scold, and quote Scripture? Do they reciprocate your openness and try to make you feel comfortable by sharing little secrets of their own? Are they generous with their love and caring, or do they withhold it? How faithful are they?

- Your friends are your spiritual fellows.
- Share all your fears and wishes with them.
- Confess all your wrongdoing to them.
- Hear their fears, wishes, and confessions.

The relationship of people with God will determine their relationship with you. The Bible says, *Do not be yoked together with unbelievers. For what do righteousness and wickedness have in common? Or what fellowship can light have with darkness?* (2 Cor. 6:14, NIV) Stay away from wicked people. They can infect you psychologically unless you approach them with the intention of helping them become believers. The Bible says, *Blessed is the man who does not walk in the counsel of the wicked or stand in the way of sinners.* (Ps. 1:1–2, NIV)

Stretch out your hands and infuse yourself into your friend's world without worrying about overreaching. Those at the beginning stages of the spiritual journey need to see you practice love, compassion, justice, fairness, kindness, and forgiveness. If you are a novice, others need to see you witnessing. Spirituality is not an isolated existence. It grows within relationships and it matures and solidifies in full view of your spiritual fellows. Of course, you may be observed by congregation members. You will be measured, using the same criteria, as to whether you'll make a good friend, a spiritual fellow.

Show all congregants affection, love, trustworthiness, gentleness, and an abundance of caring. The Bible directs, *Be sympathetic, kind, humble, gentle, and patient.* (Col. 3:12, GWT) Some people think that caring for others takes something from themselves. They believe psychological energy is a limited commodity and that directing too much of this energy to others will deplete it, leaving little for their own needs. To them, caring is similar to cutting up a pie: the whole is diminished with each slice given away. In such people you see a distancing from others, a self-protective shield. But distancing starves the soul. The best protection from self-depletion is the all-encompassing circle of caring. Caring and compassion aren't like finite circles of pie, decreasing with each slice of love given. They are infinite circles: the more that is given away, the wider the circles become, allowing more pieces of the pie to be delivered.

# EXERCISES FOR PSYCHO-SPIRITUAL FITNESS

### THE WISDOM LEARNED FROM THE BIBLE

*God wants me to trust only my fellow believers.*

### MEDITATIVE EXERCISE OF SELF-REVELATION

*Have I been too closely associating with unbelievers?*

### PRAYER EXERCISE OF GRATITUDE

*Dear God, thank You for Your trust in me.*

### INTENTIONAL EXERCISE OF SPIRITUAL REALIGNMENT

*I'll be trusting and trustworthy with my spiritual friends.*

## TALK ABOUT YOUR FAITH

*I will declare your name to my brothers; in the congregation*
*I will praise you.*

Ps. 22:22 (NIV)

The easiest path to finding a spiritual friend is to talk about your faith with him or her without any discomfort. Talk about your salvation, without any embarrassment. It is in the Bible: *I am not ashamed of the Gospel, because it is the power of God for the salvation of everyone who believes.* (Rom. 1:16, NIV)

An elderly man complained of not having friends: "I am afraid to talk about my religion and beliefs to other people." Unless people share their faith with you, you'll never get to know them. Equally, unless you share your faith with others, they'll never know you. Only by sharing faith can we penetrate the innermost recesses of each other's souls, and it is only there that our true selves can be found. Embrace others as we all form one spiritual body and kneel in front of the truly spiritual friend. Such kneeling will keep you in good standing.

## FAILINGS OF FRIENDSHIPS ARE NATURAL

*When I want to do good, I don't. And when I try*
*not to do wrong, I do it anyway.*

Rom. 7:19 (NLT)

We feel bad, guilty, and inferior because of the notion that humans are innately good and do good things. While this is true, it's not all that simple. We are vulnerable creatures. If left to our own devices, we are tempted to cheat, lie, brag, and indulge in other excesses. We will do all the selfish and wrong things imaginable. As noted in the quotation above from Paul's letter to the Romans, our weaknesses are always there, although our intentions may be good. In brief, humans are fallible by nature.

The idea of infallibility belongs to early childhood expectations of our parents. In time, we realize that our parents are quite fallible, and once the family fails our projected image, we transfer our fantasies and expectations onto our friends, our newly found alternative family.

By seeing others as infallible, you set yourself up for frustration and disappointment. In reality you will be subjected to the shortcomings and betrayals of friends and other intimates. Your patience and your ability to forgive will be tested again and again. The Bible says, *A man's wisdom gives him patience; it is to his glory to overlook an offense.* (Prov. 19:11, NIV)

How we react when a friend fails us—whether we feel sadness or rage—can be traced back to our earliest relationship with our mother. In the mother-child relationship, the child can't be responsible for helping the mother recover from her empathic failures. Fallout from a friend's failure, however, requires mutuality of adulthood. To spare friends embarrassment and shame, we need to lift the burden of failures from their shoulders. "I know you're my friend," said a fellow to his friend after being told that the friend would miss his upcoming wedding. "I know you would have liked to have been present at my wedding. When you said you couldn't, that was enough for me, because I know you would have if you could have."

- Expect fallibility in your friends.
- Be loyal to your friends.
- Don't demand loyalty from your friends.

Loyalty is the cornerstone of trusting relationships. Without the confidence we find in loyalty, we are bereft in our insecure existence. But loyalty cannot be demanded and is valuable only when spontaneously offered. Any solicitation of loyalty betrays its nature. Loyalty is not a transaction; it cannot be traded for money, promises, gratitude, charity, or pity. Loyalty cannot even be exchanged with loyalty. It may be a two-way street, but not necessarily. Offer your friend your loyalty without demanding or expecting reciprocity. It either exists or it doesn't.

Loyalty is multifaceted: It is emotional—the loyalty of values; ideological—the loyalty of principles; spiritual—the loyalty of faith. Betrayal of any one of these loyalties may challenge your beliefs, your commitment to relationships or to a cause. Betraying these loyalties may even shake the very sense of being in spiritually vulnerable persons. But God tells us betrayals (personal, ideological, or spiritual) shouldn't shake our beliefs in human relationships or our principles. *You must make allowance for each other's faults.* (Col. 3:13, NLT) If anything, betrayals of any sort should strengthen your commitment and determination to believe in the wholesomeness of your spiritual relationships.

Don't expect absolute loyalty. If you tend to do so, you need to question your expectation. Jesus was abandoned by his disciples. Even Peter explicitly and repeatedly rejected his relationship with Jesus. Why do you expect yourself to be immune from betrayal? The best way of securing the ultimate loyalty is to anticipate and accept betrayal, like Jesus.

## SPIRITUAL FRIENDS FORGIVE AND ARE FORGIVEN

*Do not say, "I'll do to him as he has done to me;*
*I'll pay that man back for what he did."*

Prov. 24:29 (NIV)

Your relationships with others need not be based on agreeing on every issue. In fact, such concurrence is either a manifestation of doctrinal compliance or insincerity. Some dogmatic individuals impose their "infallible" views on psychologically vulnerable friends. They demand not only total acceptance of their opinions, but also testimonials. Others, who are not taken in by the irrefutability of such dogmatists may, nevertheless, and insincerely, go along for reasons of their own.

God wants you to agree with your spiritual fellows on the nature of your relationship but not necessarily on a topic at hand. Unity is not uniformity. The conflicts among spiritual fellows should be limited to the content of the subject. In certain matters either you or one of your fellows may be better informed and even be an authority on specific subject. But there is great difference between knowledge based on experience and assertion based on arrogance. Being knowledgeable or wise comes with an attitude of humility.

A spiritual person never allows a relationship to deteriorate for the sake of being proven right. You are not immune from wrongdoing. Whenever you are wrong or hurtful, don't try to deny it or make lame excuses for it: just confess and accept the consequences, including being forgiven. To offer and receive forgiveness is one of the essential elements of spiritual relations. Being human means having faults and flaws, making errors—including moral ones—and being fallible.

When a friend's behavior hurts you, do not think the behavior was specifically intended to target you. The friend is acting this way for his or her own reason. Usually the hurtful tendency to err is caused by ignorance. Christ on the cross asks forgiveness for His betrayers, saying to His Father, *"They know not what they do."* (Luke 23:34, KJV) Only those who know God know what they do. You must forgive friends, no matter how seemingly unforgivable their behavior. Forgiveness, incidentally, is not forgiving a single sin or error. It is having a permanent predisposition to forgive. It is a way of being within a relationship.

Forgiveness is also an essential element of faith. If you believe in forgiveness, you believe in the fellowship of humanity. As long as transgressors demonstrate genuine remorse, repentance, and a wish to undo the harm, forgive them and forget the whole event. This is real forgiveness. By forgiving our fellows in faith, we earn the forgiveness of God.

# EXERCISES FOR PSYCHO-SPIRITUAL FITNESS

### THE WISDOM LEARNED FROM THE BIBLE

*God wants me to make allowance
for my friends' faults.*

### MEDITATIVE EXERCISE
### OF SELF-REVELATION

*Have I been accepting the fallibility
of my friends?*

### PRAYER EXERCISE OF GRATITUDE

*Dear God, thank You for Your forgiveness.*

### INTENTIONAL EXERCISE
### OF SPIRITUAL REALIGNMENT

*I'll overlook the offenses of my friends.*

## SEEK COMPASSIONATE TRUTHFULNESS

*For whatever is in your heart determines what you say.*

Matt. 12:34 (NLT)

We all struggle with the dilemma of being truthful or being compassionate with our intimates. The Bible tells us that *in the end, people appreciate frankness more than flattery.* (Prov. 28:23, NLT) But God cautions us to make sure that what we say comes from the heart, that we have good intentions and nothing else. Being brutally honest with friends is not being intimate with them. Good judgment and compassion must temper what we say to others. Every person carries some little lie (a story conjured during formative years) in his or her soul. The stories are at times fantastic, such as pretending to come from a noble family; at times innocent, such as exaggerating the size of a fish caught on a trip or being the favorite child of a parent, grandparent, or teacher. Sometimes the stories are less self-congratulatory and more self-pitying or self-derogatory. They recount abuse, being an outcast, or being poor and isolated. There are as many such lies as there are souls.

These stories find themselves a corner in people's personalities and become their life lies. These lies get played and replayed as variations of the original stories in contemporary relationships. Confronting your friends with their life lies is unnecessary and hurtful. These lies are very much a part of them; in fact, pulling the lies out of them may damage the structure of their souls. Don't throw too much light on your friends, even though you may need to illuminate their lives. Contemplate your friends for self-revelation. Receive what is offered; value it as it is. Knowingly accept a friend's counterfeit coin, but do not pass it on.

- Be truthful with your friends.
- Be compassionate when telling the truth.
- Don't seek vices in your friends.
- Seek and discover the virtues of your friends.

Try to discover your friends' virtues but not their vices. Don't focus on the vices if you notice them. We all have imperfections and peculiarities; they are part of our makeup. Whatever the reason for their existence, peculiarities give our personalities distinct patterns, colors, and textures. They are intricately woven into our being. Trying to remove them is like pulling at an errant thread in a sweater: if you keep pulling at the thread, you risk unraveling the whole sweater. As a friend, make sure the errant threads don't catch onto something and become more unraveled. Try to weave the threads back into the sweater if your friends recruit you to do so. That is the mending required for friendship.

# EXERCISES FOR PSYCHO-SPIRITUAL FITNESS

### THE WISDOM LEARNED FROM THE BIBLE

*God wants me to speak from my heart.*

### MEDITATIVE EXERCISE
### OF SELF-REVELATION

*Have I been compassionate in my truthfulness?*

### PRAYER EXERCISE OF GRATITUDE

*Dear God, thank You for Your truth.*

### INTENTIONAL EXERCISE
### OF SPIRITUAL REALIGNMENT

*I'll focus on the virtues of my friends.*

*[The Bible] is the best book that was ever or ever will be known in the world, . . . because it teaches you the best lessons by which any human creature who tries to be truthful and faithful to duty can possibly be guided.*

Charles Dickens, Letter to his son, September 1868

# CHAPTER VIII

# STRIVING FOR
# A GODLY COMMUNITY

*You are citizens along with all of
God's holy people. You are members
of God's family.*

Eph. 2:19 (NLT)

Part of the anxiety we feel today is related to the abandonment of our spiritual connections. The ability of the human mind to process information has far outstripped its capacity to meet its visceral needs for restraint. We have declared ourselves masters of nature and patrons of the Houses of God, and we hope to gain power over both. When we sever ties with God and congregation, however, we become spiritually and morally alone. And this aloneness unleashes all too human weaknesses: pride, envy, gluttony, lust, anger, greed, and sloth.

Unconsciously, we all long for submission to a higher power as we longed for powerful parents when we were children. Those who do not subordinate themselves to God usually submit to false gods and ideals. The rationale to free people from religiosity—the dogmatic misapplication of God's word—has morphed into an equally misdirected effort to free ourselves from religion. We do not need freedom from religion but we do need freedom to have faith. There is only one eternal shelter and that is, as the Bible says, *none other than the house of God.* (Gen. 28:17, NLT)

In the house of God you are in the company of other faithful congregants, who are also free to believe, and God will be there too. He reassures us: *"For where two or three have gathered together in my name, I am there in their midst."* (Matt. 18:20, NASB)

Our extended biological family connects us to our personal past and to our ephemeral future. It tells us where we came from and to whom we belong, and teaches us how to nourish ourselves with love. Our spiritual family, our congregation, connects us to our historic, mythic past and to our eternal future. It tells us who we were and who we are and also teaches us how to sustain ourselves with faith.

Our social character strengthens our sense of self and protects us from deviating from fundamental values. But should we stray too far from these essential values, our spiritual family validates the confidence that God will restore us. Together our extended and spiritual families strengthen our loves and our beliefs and deeply ground us. *God makes us one body . . . connected to each other.* (Rom. 12:5, GWT)

Religion is the worldview shared with our spiritual family. Faith provides meaning to our lives. Religion provides us a congregation with whom we share faith. In a congregation we grow deep roots and affix ourselves to the communality of the fellowship and spiritual power embodied within it. Our longing for wholeness and security of belonging fulfilled, we confirm our faith in a communal matrix.

## ANCHOR ON YOUR SPIRITUAL COMMUNITY

*Each part gets its meaning from the body as a whole.*

Rom. 12:4 (MSG)

As the ocean exists in the togetherness of all its drops of water, the spiritual community exists in the togetherness of all its members. Spiritual existence is spiritual *co*existence. You cannot make sense of the how or why of being while in isolation. You cannot even conjure up the idea of the Creator when you are alone. Only in a spiritual community does faith gather strength and only in a spiritual community is faith guarded undefiled. Devoid of a spiritual community, you have no yardstick with which to measure yourself, never mind God.

Secular society is organized lovelessness. Its members are burdened by the weight of being unable to trust or believe in the compassion of others. In a spiritual society the shared love of God lightens burdens, and there is always someone to trust and someone from whom you can receive compassion. Not belonging to a congregation eventually leads to isolation. Estranged from fellow beings, the isolated person tends to become spiritually impoverished. Unrestrained by the advice, encouragement, teaching, and praise—and even admonishment—of community members, the spiritually disconnected person, like an amputated limb, cannot survive.

- Ground yourself in one place.
- Weave yourself into your community.
- Spread your roots deep and wide.

Self-isolation is equally harmful to the family and the community. Continuing the analogy above, a body may survive without a limb but it will be handicapped. A community is at its best when all its members are intact in faith and functioning in spiritual harmony with each other. Spiritual harmony encompasses not only peaceful and soulful existence but also a meaningful existence. Conversely, it is immensely difficult to formulate meaning for your life in isolation. The meaning in your individual life can be extracted only from the meaning of the whole. The Bible says, *Each part gets its meaning from the body as a whole.* (Rom. 12:4, MSG)

One important element that the body as a whole has is continuity. As humans, we crave the continuity of the past and our link with the future. Religion unites us in that yearning and promises us eternal and ultimate continuity. Religion is our collective framework, shaping our personal past, present, and future. Religion is our collective philosophy. It anchors our personal convictions and our wondering. In religion, we become part of the continuity of the eternal.

# EXERCISES FOR PSYCHO-SPIRITUAL FITNESS

### THE WISDOM LEARNED FROM THE BIBLE

*God wants me to be interested*
*in the lives of others.*

### MEDITATIVE EXERCISE OF SELF-REVELATION

*Have I been too preoccupied with my*

*own interests?*

### PRAYER EXERCISE OF GRATITUDE

*Dear God, thank You for being interested in me.*

### INTENTIONAL EXERCISE OF SPIRITUAL REALIGNMENT

*I'll call or visit a member*
*of my congregation today.*

## THE DEEPER YOUR ROOTS, THE HIGHER YOUR BRANCHES WILL BE

*No branch can bear fruit by itself; it must remain in the vine.*

John 15:4 (NIV)

Spiritual roots can be compared to the roots of bushes and trees. Bushes tend to have shallow roots, and as a result, they don't grow very high. Trees, like the oak, grow their roots deep and spread them wide, and as a result, they grow very tall and strong. Bushes, with their shallow roots, are easily uprooted; deep-rooted trees can survive major storms. If you are not deeply rooted in the ground of your community, you will experience a minor stress as destabilizing. When you are well rooted, you can withstand major stresses. You can obtain the security you crave only by sinking your roots deeply into the community.

Without God you are unsheltered. The greater your attempt to define yourself as an independent entity, the more you realize how vulnerable you are. Successfully identifying your boundaries will leave you feeling totally alone and exposed.

We associate adulthood with independence. The statement "He/she is very independent" is considered to be high praise, and to some extent, it is. A dependent person is not considered a fully mature individual. Maturity that culminates as a well-defined sense of self requires self-sufficiency, self-respect, emotional self-containment, and even a personal philosophy. If a person's sense of self is rigidly adhered to, however, that person will find the process of maturation an isolated and disconnected existence. God does not want us to make maturity or individuality the final points of arrival. He wants us to depend on Him and be sheltered in Him.

Independence without community leaves you vulnerable to stress. If you do not have strong connections to your community, your loss of health, job, or spouse will make you tumble. If you establish strong roots in your community you can grow to your highest potential. You have to remain there, however, to grow roots.

Promises of opportunities away from your community will displace you, depriving you and your family of irreplaceable connections. By uprooting yourself from your spiritual ground, you excommunicate yourself. Even if you are welcomed with open arms into a new community, you are a stranger without historical mooring. Can you reestablish roots? Yes, of course; transplanted trees go through shock, though eventually they may thrive even more. But the simplest path for personal and spiritual growth is to make a fully committed effort to stay within your community and to weave yourself into it.

Weaving yourself into a community doesn't mean mindless immersion in it. The Bible says, *Don't become so well adjusted to your culture that you fit into it without even thinking.* (Rom. 12:2, MSG) While you may make every effort to belong to the secular community you live in, you must remain in constant touch with your spiritual community. In the secular world, you run the risk of being pulled into a way of living that is contrary to your spiritual habits. Compromising your religious values is not adapting; it is forfeiting your soul. Instead of abandoning your belief system, assert your faith with even greater strength and determination.

## SPIRITUAL COMMUNION IS KNIT
## ONE STITCH AT A TIME

> *Their hearts may be encouraged, having been knit*
> *together in love, and attaining to all the wealth that comes*
> *from the full assurance of understanding, resulting in a*
> *true knowledge of God's mystery.*

Col. 2:2 (NASB)

Integrating yourself into the community is like knitting a sweater; it's done one stitch at a time. It is a slow, steady, and careful process. Although your overall goal is clear, you don't focus on the whole but pursue each action independently for its own sake. Narrow your attention to one stitch and the next, making sure that each is well placed. Thousands of such stitches will one day be a sweater.

Some find knitting boring and would rather buy a sweater instead of making one. You cannot belong to a community by buying it, though it is frequently attempted. Some people give large gifts to schools with the purpose of getting their children accepted; they make donations to museums to get their names plastered on the walls; they contribute sums of money to parks so the parks will be named after them. Knitting yourself into a community means offering not only money but donating your time, energy, and attention. It means being interested in the lives of others. This may include volunteering at a school that your children don't attend, planting bushes or clearing debris from a park, offering to serve in a local nursing home or a firehouse, coaching youngsters in sports or singing in the choir of your house of worship. The Bible says, *Do not be interested only in your own life, but be interested in the lives of others.* (Phil. 2:4,

NCV) Enlightenment is the cultivation of your fellows' gardens.

- Partake of collective myths and rituals.
- Fix a time.
- Fix a place.
- Fix a method.

"I believe in God, but I don't go to church," said an educated, lonely woman. "I have no patience with or interest in the obsessive rituals of the church. I have even less interest in ancient stories, symbols, and myths." She was lonely because she had isolated herself from past generations by rejecting their beliefs and myths. Further, she had estranged herself from the present generation by choosing not to participate in the ritual enactment of those ancient myths.

The congregation confirms our collective longing for God. While worshipping and praying alone is an inner communion with God, worshipping and praying with others is an outer communion with God. When you say "Amen" after your prayer in solitude, you emphasize your devotion. When you are praying with others, your "Amen" is the expression of agreement among you *all true and sure.* (1 Cor. 14:16, NIV) You are seeking not only God, but also confirmation of your search.

Events of public worship such as rites, sacraments, ceremonies, and liturgies are as important as private devotional exercises. When you listen to this type of public worship it sounds like a harmonious choir singing in the same key to the same rhythm. When such synchrony occurs among a large number of worshippers, the whole house of worship resonates so powerfully with their spirit that even the most skeptical are moved to kneel and affirm their devotion. It is written in the Bible: *And when they had prayed, the place where they were assembled together was shaken; and they were all filled with the Holy Spirit* . . . (Acts 4:31, NKJV)

Our myths and rituals are far from being obsessive in nature, as that lonely woman asserted. They are concrete manifestations of our beliefs, and they are not restricted to religious ceremonies but exist in every aspect of our lives. These rituals bring a sense of the sacred to ordinary life and provide a meaningful bond among us. When words fail to express the meaning of our deepest selves, symbols take over, registering the silent devotional language that serves our communion. When you are immersed in the spiritual community, even without your full awareness, you'll be satiated with devotion. There is an old saying, "The fish is never thirsty."

Those who insist that believing in God is sufficient miss the opportunity to belong and to grow their spirit in fellowship. They also miss the opportunity to be sheltered in the House of God. These modern secularists or quasi-spiritual people have lost their bonds, their structure, and their history. Now, alone and homeless, they improvise a personal life philosophy and shuffle their soul from one inadequate shelter to another.

# EXERCISES FOR PSYCHO-SPIRITUAL FITNESS

### THE WISDOM LEARNED FROM THE BIBLE

*God wants me to be a member of His family.*

### MEDITATIVE EXERCISE OF SELF-REVELATION

*Have I been sufficiently involved in my congregation to call it my family?*

### PRAYER EXERCISE OF GRATITUDE

*Dear God, thank You for including me in Your family.*

### INTENTIONAL EXERCISE OF SPIRITUAL REALIGNMENT

*This week I'll attend the gatherings of God's family.*

## DELIVER YOUR MINISTRY OF WITNESS

*I will follow You, Lord, and become your disciple.*

Luke 9:61 (AMP)

You have practical and ministerial responsibilities to your house of worship and its ministers. If you are called, go and be obedient. Engage with clergy as they interact with the secular world and help them with their temporal affairs. In your ministry of witness, assist in the sanctification of the world by spreading the word of God.

- Share your faith with others.
- Share the goodness of God with others.
- Serve your house of worship and its ministries.
- Serve members of your congregation.

Spirituality is your right and privilege, a sweet repository, a heavy burden to accept joyfully. It is a source of harmony in the universe and is the regulator of hearts and souls. It is the reverence to and the espousal of moral ideals. Spirituality is also a duty: you must bring all of God's goodness to other people in ever-extending circles, in the way a stone cast on water generates outward-radiating waves.

God wants you to consecrate your personal life for humanitarian ends. The Bible says, *Whenever you have the opportunity, you should do good to everyone.* (Gal. 6:10, NLT) Help others; be compassionate. Personal suffering generates helplessness, while compassion—suffering with others—is powerful. If you are compassionate, you'll be rewarded by "helper's calm," the most extraordinary sense of abandon. Being compassionate comes easily to the faithful. The love of God automatically transforms one's passion into compassion. We all have a passion for something: reading, playing an instrument, gardening, decorating, sports, collecting. Whatever the nature of your passion, it is geared to satisfying yourself. As healthy and ethical as a passion might be, it still serves your own specific interests.

The ultimate satisfaction—a feeling of exaltation—comes from transforming these passions into compassion that serves the communal interest. This transformation of passion into compassion, for example, may take the form of tutoring less fortunate youngsters in the community or providing them with books and even a library. Compassion is a kind of inter-generational altruism. We read books written or bought by others and eat fruit whose trees were planted by others. Though compassion means "suffering with," it is also "enjoying with." Compassion is the communal and intergenerational glue that holds us together. It means belonging to the family of God and doing His family's chores gratefully.

As Psalm 146:7–8 (MSG) proclaims: *God . . . feeds the hungry . . . and gives sight to the blind.* God presides over all these and similar acts and uses us to deliver them. We are his hands and feet in ordinary life and His voice in the vernacular.


## YOU ARE AT HOME IN YOUR CONGREGATION

*[God] . . . called you out of darkness into His wonderful light.*

1 Peter 2:9 (NIV)

"My therapist says that my religion has made me neurotic," asserted a young unmarried woman. If anything, religion may have saved her from becoming psychotic. Religion is not a neurosis, filling our minds with illusions. It is a normalizer, a regulator of behavior. In fact, religion restrains our neuroses. It is the antidote against powerful sexual and aggressive drives, and it is our collective weapon against indulging in these drives and becoming slaves to them. The estrangement from God is the cause of these destructive drives. We are not at the mercy of unconscious drives when we are at the mercy of God. Every moral failure is a sign of spiritual isolation.

There are many excuses given for not joining a congregation. Some of them: "I don't have time." "It's too far to travel." "The sermons are too long and boring." "I believe in God, that's enough." The worst excuse for not joining a congregation is considering it "not good enough." A congregation is like a family; it is a spiritual fellowship. There are no good or bad or smart or dumb congregations. A congregation is what it is: all of us together, good and bad, rich and poor, smart and dumb. Embrace members of your congregation with kind acceptance, generosity of heart, and genuine respect. The Bible says, *God's people should be bighearted and courteous.* (Titus 3:2, MSG)

When joining a new community, you naturally may be hesitant initially about engaging the community members. People who remain unengaged lack trust in spiritual fellowship. It wouldn't be surprising to find out that these people are equally disengaged from their other communities, including from their co-workers at work, and perhaps, their families.

There are those who, after initial reticence, quickly warm up and fully engage others. These are the people that any congregation loves to keep. The Bible says, *Many are invited, but few of those are chosen to stay.* (Matt. 22:14, GWT) Try to be one of them. You'll see how everyone reciprocates and in no time you'll all behave as if you have known each other for a long time. In fact, your spiritual fellowship is a transferable trust and a transferable affection. If you come from a spiritual home, you'll easily enter other spiritual homes. If you were a spiritual fellow in one congregation, you'll meet many spiritual fellows in other communions.

Of course, it isn't feasible or necessary to get to know everyone intimately. God tells us to behave toward others as if we have the intention and the desire to get to know them. These "strangers" are known, loved, and trusted by someone to whom they are lovable and trustworthy. We tend to distrust strangers until they prove their trustworthiness to us. We are suspicious of their intentions and we attribute the worst qualities to them because "unknown" translates to "untrustworthy." Of course, the reverse also occurs: others don't trust us either. They project undesirable qualities and unworthiness onto us. Psychological doors begin to lock and we build big walls to protect our impenetrable selves.

If you approach someone with an attitude of bias and mistrust, you'll be received with a similar bad-faith attitude, and your assumptions will be confirmed. If you encounter others with good faith and consider them trustworthy, you will, most likely, generate similar sentiments toward yourself. Even if this doesn't happen, remain on course: one failing (or ten) shouldn't shake your faith in the goodness of God's creatures. As part of a well-known prayer attributed to St. Francis goes, "Where there is hatred, let me sow love."

- Expect to be well received.
- Take people to joyful places.
- Pursue only the love of the spiritual.
- It is best not to be liked by the non-spiritual.

## LET GOD REMEMBER YOUR GOOD DEEDS

*My God will remember these good things that I have done.*

Neh. 13:14 (CEV)

Every trace of good will on your part reflects the goodness of Providence. Every act of generosity on your part resonates with God's values. Both are imbedded in His message: *"All of us share one loaf."* (1 Cor. 10:17, GWT) The only authentic generosity is a spiritual one—giving unconditionally, without expectation of reciprocity or even thanks. Don't attempt to immortalize yourself by attaching your good deeds to rewards. No matter how valuable and needed the gift, it should never bind the receiver with chains of gratitude. Coveting others' gratitude is worse than being close-fisted.

Giving money and other goods to the needy is not generosity in the strict sense of the word; it is the mediation of God's bounty to others. How many times have you seen shattered statues or long-forgotten pedestals inscribed with names that no one remembers? Ultimately, we are all anonymous. Only God will remember our names and our deeds. We are immortal only in serving God.

## STRIVE TO BE LIKED ONLY BY LOVING PEOPLE

*Show special love for God's people.*

1 Peter 2:17 (CEV)

No matter how much you love others and how good and kind and well-meaning a person you are, you may find that some people do not like you. This is puzzling because you may have done nothing to deserve their dislike. You may, in fact, go out of your way to show them how nice you are. Interestingly enough, the more you try, the less likely you'll succeed. Your very attempt will perpetuate rejection and a vicious circle will ensue. There is no exit from that interplay, though the person whose favor you're trying to gain may give infrequent and irregular crumbs of approval to maintain the relationship. The truth is, total hopelessness in such a relationship is mercifully less torturing.

In telling us *love others as you love yourself* (Gal. 5:14, MSG), the Bible is urging an offering to all, but a group deserving our "special love" is identified: *Show special love for God's people.* Equally important, you should want to be loved by God's people. You should want to be loved only by loving people who accept (or reject) others on the basis of their spirituality, ethics, and morality. Those who are spiritual will extend their love to you the same way that you do to them, without expectation of reciprocation. They love and they are loving people, period.

Welcome rejection from unloving, unfaithful, unspiritual people who negate others purely on the basis of their own convoluted needs. Reject the love of people who are selfish, greedy, and who lack compassion and integrity. Their affection is deceptive and manipulative. Being unloved or disliked by such non-spiritual people brings you closer to real love.

# EXERCISES FOR PSYCHO-SPIRITUAL FITNESS

### THE WISDOM LEARNED FROM THE BIBLE

*God wants me to show love for His people.*

### MEDITATIVE EXERCISE OF SELF-REVELATION

*Have I shown a special love to those I believe are God's people?*

### PRAYER EXERCISE OF GRATITUDE

*Dear God, thank You for Your special love for me.*

### INTENTIONAL EXERCISE OF SPIRITUAL REALIGNMENT

*Today I'll express my love to some members of my congregation.*

## STAY HOME, YOUNG PEOPLE

*"My wayward children," says the Lord, "come back to me,
and I will heal your wayward hearts."*

Jer. 3:22 (NLT)

The nineteenth-century directive, "Go West, young man" served its purpose a long time ago. We've circled the globe. Now going farther west means circling back east. A motto for our time is: "Stay put!"

Stay put, especially if you live in a small town or in a city of manageable size that retains the soul of a small town. Going to the "Big Apple" or "Tinseltown" or the "Windy City" is considered courageous and ambitious. "Get out of your cocoon and spread your wings, face challenges, push yourself to your limits," well-meaning life coaches tell us. But it would be helpful if these coaches would remind themselves of the fate of cut flowers. Of course, there are greater professional opportunities and cultural enhancements in big cities. The worlds of entertainment, newspapers and other media, science and education, commerce and banking, and almost any other field are concentrated in large cities. Theaters, museums, and other cultural institutions compete for your attention. You'll find yourself entertained, educated, stimulated, and at times even inundated with opportunities and cultural events in a large city.

You'll be exposed to many and diverse religions, cultures, languages, and more. While this seems enriching, it is also diluting. Striving for "up and wide" interferes with growing "down and deep." Your belief system, your morality, and even your sanity will be challenged. You'll drift from one event to another in a frenzy of activity, never staying anywhere long enough to deepen any one of your experiences. You'll rarely meet people like yourself for self-validation. Rather, you'll be bombarded with questions: "Why do you pray before each meal?" "You call home every week?" You'll question yourself.

In a large city, when you come home at the end of the day you might find yourself totally alone. If you live in an apartment building, you may not know the names of your neighbors. The day you move in, it is unlikely you will find someone to bring you a welcoming pot roast or a cake, though you may get scolding looks from your neighbors because you're making too much noise moving furniture.

Large cities are heterogeneous communities where every belief under the sun is reflected in its people. There are no norms to adopt. You may choose a way of dressing, working, having sex, philosophizing, or worshipping one month, and try something else the next month. No one questions; no one cares. You don't have to adhere to existing mores; instead, you make your own choices and become your own point of reference. As desirable as that may sound, it is also destabilizing, like building a house on a float instead of cementing it onto a foundation.

If you live in a big city you need to find like-minded people of similar backgrounds and create your own small community. No matter how small the congregation, it still satisfies the need of people to belong to something.

Spiritual enlightenment may occur in isolation to a few who are blessed with a quantum leap of faith. In fact, such leaps of enlightenment invariably occur in solitude. For the rest of us, living with our fellow believers is needed for a devotional life. The long-praised idea of the melting pot may be useful for integrating newcomers with each other and the

established community. It may help newcomers economi-
cally and socially and even give them a new identity, but the
pot also melts away their original identity that is embedded
in their religions and cultures. Iron, copper, tin, bronze,
gold, silver, may be blended into new metals. The amalgams
may be shinier, more flexible, and even more valuable than
the original, but they are no longer the same.

## THE SOUL MATURES BEST IN ITS OWN SOIL

*Remember, you aren't feeding the root; the root is feeding you.*

Rom. 11:18 (MSG)

Transplanted vines don't do well unless planted in soil similar to their soil of origin. Of course, it is best to cultivate
vines where they belong. Sometimes we do not have a choice
as to where we settle. When circumstances force you to
move from your home community, go without fear but keep
your devotional life intact wherever you go. The Bible says,
*Be strong and of good courage; do not be afraid, nor be dis-
mayed, for the Lord, your God is with you wherever you go.*
(Josh. 1:9, NKJV) A God-loving person makes him or herself at home in every climate and country.

The smaller the community, the easier it is to know people and to be known by them. In a tightly knit community,
you have a sense of total belonging. You know innately the
rules of the community, its prohibitions and expectations.
You don't need to be told, "This is not done here!" You
know that you don't blow the car horn at three in the morning because the car in front of you is hesitating at the inter-
section. You respect the elderly, and you show up and
participate in the local house of worship.

Whether in a small town or a small community within a big city, you need to participate enthusiastically in the activities of your "tribe." Enjoy its birthdays and weddings; take part in school games and performances and in the election of its officers, and also suffer with your tribe during illnesses, after accidents, and at funerals.

## MARRY THE GIRL OR BOY NEXT DOOR

*Swear . . . that you . . . will go to my country and*
*my own relatives and get a wife for my son Isaac.*

Genesis 24:3–4 (NIV)

Each "tribe" has its own rules of conduct, extending from worship to celebration, from weddings to funerals, from working to leisure activities. Rules of conduct even encompass daily habits, including eating or avoiding certain foods, or engaging in certain sports or entertainments and not others. If you want to feel at home, marry someone from your tribe. The girl-next-door image frequently is used to describe a familiar goodness but an unexciting marriage prospect. But the excitement factor is the least likely predictor for happiness and longevity in a relationship. In fact, marrying the girl or boy next door is one of the most reliable indices for the continuity of spiritual homes.

If you marry someone outside your tribe, you and your partner will have to negotiate every step along the path of your marriage. You'll spend more time trying to reconcile your differences than attending to matters at hand. Even if you agree about a particular subject one day, the next day you may face some variation of the issue that requires negotiation. Nothing will come easily or spontaneously. There is no implicit understanding or silent recognition of sameness. If anything, implicit and explicit misunderstandings will permeate the relationship. This is not the kind of effort that fosters a stable union in marriage, nor does it foster betterment through collaboration. It is establishing the starting line, again and again.

In out-of-tribe marriages, long, arduous negotiations and fights deplete everyone. One partner eventually gives in from sheer fatigue and lets the other take over. The compromised partner usually feels demoralized and depressed, losing the important part of himself or herself that was defined by the tribe. The extent of the compromise determines the damage to the person's soul, and eventually the person becomes spiritually impoverished.

- Associate with fellows of your tribe.
- Marry within the tribe.
- Cultivate your tribal qualities.
- Cultivate the qualities of your tribe.

If you weave yourself further into your tribal community through marriage, you'll be freed from time-consuming negotiations. You'll know where you stand in every aspect of your life and effortlessly move from one arena to another. Having common morals, ethics, rituals, and a sense of oneness with your spiritual partner will simplify your life and make it joyful.

# THE GROUND IS BEST FERTILIZED BY THOSE WHO DWELL ON IT

*Be very sure now, you who have been trained to a self-sufficient maturity, that you enter into a generous common life with those who have trained you, sharing all the good things that you have and experience.*

Gal. 6:6 (MSG)

You must actively help your tribe flourish. Your community is your ground and you begin when you are planted on it. After you grow deep roots, you can find water, grow tall, catch sun, mature, and bear fruit. But you must fertilize your ground; this means taking care of the parks and water system of your community; becoming active in the campaign against air pollution; volunteering at schools, hospitals and newspapers in your town; and strengthening your house of worship. It means giving. Such devotional giving will not deplete you, but will replenish you. The Bible says: *Give and it will be given to you. A good measure, pressed down, shaken together and running over, will be poured into your lap.* (Luke 6:38, NIV)

Devotional giving isn't an act of charity but a responsibility, the fulfillment of communal duty. Fertilizing your ground means serving the needs of the community and fully adopting its values and ethics. It means being concerned for the community's safety, integrity, and well-being.

In belonging to a community you immediately inherit the benefits of the work of previous generations. You walk on the streets they paved, cross the bridges they built, work in factories they constructed, read in the libraries they founded, sleep safely because of the police and fire departments they established, get medical care in the hospitals they opened, and send your children to schools they created. Reap with gratitude the crop that others have sown. There is absolutely no sin in doing so, provided that you also joyfully sow a new harvest for others to reap. Only then will you have established and secured your spiritual continuity.

# EXERCISES FOR PSYCHO-SPIRITUAL FITNESS

## THE WISDOM LEARNED FROM THE BIBLE

*God wants me to serve Him*
*by serving my congregation.*

## MEDITATIVE EXERCISE OF SELF-REVELATION

*Have I been an obedient servant to God?*

## PRAYER EXERCISE OF GRATITUDE

*Dear God, thank You for choosing me to serve.*

## INTENTIONAL EXERCISE OF SPIRITUAL REALIGNMENT

*Today I'll seek an opportunity to serve others.*

*Any group of men, however ignorant, need only to be able to read the Bible to be in possession of the ultimate, undeniable truth about almost any important question of human life.*

Everett Dean Martin, *Liberty*, 1930

# CHAPTER IX

# STRIVING FOR GODLY HARMONY

*A plain and simple life is a full life.*

Prov. 13:7 (MSG)

If you want to know about living a peaceful life, just knock on your inner doors—your real self, your innocent mind, your pure emotions, your soul. The knowledge is there, waiting to be tapped: a full, simple, and joyful life awaits you. If you pay attention to commercials, television shows, and movies, you would believe that "having it all" is what makes life full. As a society we are obsessed with our outer selves, our looks, hair, clothes, jewelry, and other ornaments. But these things don't bring inner peace. The Bible says, *Your beauty should not come from outward adornment, such as braided hair and the wearing of gold jewelry and fine clothes. Instead, it should be that of your inner self, the unfading beauty of a gentle and quiet spirit, which is of great worth in God's sight.* (1 Peter 3:3-4, NIV)

We are preoccupied equally with our bodies—our muscles, our waists, our contours. It is fine and desirable to exercise to stay fit, but it's not fine to make it an obsession. About exercise the Bible says, *Physical training is of some value, but godliness has value for all things.* (1 Tim. 4:8, NIV) It is also acceptable and desirable to be within your expected, healthy weight range, but why starve for the sake of your appearance? The Bible says about appearance, *Man looks at the outward appearance, but the Lord looks at the heart.* (1 Sam. 16:7, NIV) Imagine yourself spending as much time caring for your inner self as you do for your outer self.

Relentlessly amassing possessions, joining clubs and other organizations, and attending parties may seem like a full life, but it is only a busy life. The moment obsessive pursuits are interrupted through losses or illness, the moment you can no longer busy yourself with those preoccupations, a gigantic hole in that "full life" emerges. The emptiness that follows keeps enlarging, generating an unbearable anxiety, threatening to cause the self to cave into a vacuum.

What makes life full is simplicity—having a few intimate friends; belonging to a few organizations of genuine interest to you; having enough money to live on; possessing only things that you really need; and seeking only recognition by God.

All pleasures (whether they are related to sex, food, rest, vacation, or games) are poor substitutes for joy. Pleasures are signs of your being alive, and you are entitled to have them. But it is important not to confuse these pleasures with joy. Joy is a deep sense of satisfaction and at its best is a feeling of exaltation derived from within.

## RECOVER YOUR LOVE OF INNOCENCE

*I may understand all mysteries and have all knowledge.*
*I may even have enough faith to move mountains.*
*But if I don't have love, I am nothing.*

1 Cor. 13:2 (GWT)

Attaining a peaceful life requires living harmoniously with all of God's creations, including animals, plants, air, and water. Peace is the communion of God's creations.

Attaining a peaceful life requires recognizing that your life is a gift from God. Gratefully accept, value, respect, and enjoy this extraordinary gift. Depending on circumstances, you will find that the seeds of life unfold differently. Appreciate every being and thing, thus unfolded as gifts of God, and celebrate the uniqueness that comes from this organic growth.

Imagine being born. You leave the safety of your mother and enter a world that, until the moment of your birth, didn't exist for you. Suddenly you open your eyes to brightness and the loving smiles of your parents; a generous supply of milk is delivered to your mouth, and your mind is exposed to a bewildering array of things, sights, and sounds. You grow up and experience new challenges—education, friendships, marriage, parenthood—as a continuation of God's gift to you. At each stage of your life you'll be offered joy, pain, anxiety, despair, and excitement. Welcome it all. Life is a total package; you cannot pick and choose what you want. Live life as it is; experience its sorrows and exultations. Dip deeply into and drink from the well of life. There, in the depth of your emotions, you will witness the mysteries of life.

There is a parable of a man who willed his treasure to his only son, provided the son became a fool. When the man died, his will was brought to the town judge. But the judge couldn't execute the will because he didn't understand what the stipulation meant. The judge called the best lawyers in the town for a consultation, but then he gave up trying to make a decision after listening to the lawyers' contradictory explanations of what a "fool" meant. Finally, the judge decided to consult the village wise man. When the judge arrived at the wise man's house, he found the man crawling on his hands and knees, giving a "horsey ride" to his two-year-old son. The judge reluctantly asked the wise man what becoming a fool meant. The exhausted, breathless man managed to answer: "This, what you see."

The deceased man in the story wanted to ensure that his son would recover his innocence and cultivate a childlike sense of delight and spontaneity. So must you, if you want to inherit the treasures of life and restore your sense of wonder, puzzlement, and amazement about the world and about your being in it.

## LOVE THE WORLD

*God so loved the world . . .*

John 3:16 (NLT)

When God said, *"Let [humans] have dominion over the fish of the sea, and over the birds of the air, and over the cattle and over all the earth,"* (Gen. 1:26, NKJV) He didn't mean for us to plunder the world. While God allows humans to use his creations, He also wants us to protect the Earth and all it holds. No one species has the right to put another's existence in danger. All of God's creatures are linked to each other and serve as means to perpetuate the earth and the creatures on it. Some birds eat fish; others eat ants, insects, and other bugs. Once we are buried at the cemetery, ants and bugs eat our flesh, breaking down our bodies and returning them to the earth.

Every living thing is miraculous—ants, flowers, squirrels, bushes, birds, trees, fish, and coral. Miraculous, too, are the inanimate things of life—a seashell, a bird's nest, a streak of sun on a forsythia leaf. Each has a purpose in being. Many are useful to us, but that is not the reason they exist. At times we forget this principle of nature: every thing is an important and precious creation of God and all living beings strive toward the single goal of perpetuating life on earth. God expects us humans to minister compassionately to all things. A peaceful and joyful life means having compassion for all creation.

- Hold every creature in high regard.
- Approach all with awe and humility.
- Be harmonious with nature.
- Experience your oneness with the universe.

Human greed and carelessness have caused the extinction of many species. We have deforested the land, polluted lakes and air, and intruded into animal habitats, endangering the existence of numerous wild animals. No individual is entitled to terminate the life of another creature unless for the legitimate purpose of eating it. I use the term "legitimate" because all God's creatures are genetically programmed (and physically limited) to eat or avoid eating certain others of His creatures and creations. Humans have outmaneuvered genetics and physical limitations, and we can eat almost any of God's creatures. This is a type of "perversion of desire" that God wants us to be rid of. *Put to death . . . your . . . perversion.* (Col. 3:5, GWT)

Sometimes this human perversity destroys creatures just for the fun of it. You may see nothing wrong with stepping on a caterpillar or flicking away a ladybug. You may consider these insects unnecessary and bothersome. But if you pay close attention to them, you will see the intricacy and complexity in the details of their bodies. Watch them head toward their intended destinations. They are so exquisitely coordinated in their microscopic movements that you can just sit in awe and observe them for hours and *be filled with the Spirit.* (Eph. 5:18, NIV) You will find more to learn and more potential for spiritual restoration in the woods than you'll find in books.

## LISTEN TO THE SERMONS OF EVERY BEING

*When I see the rainbow in the clouds, I will remember the eternal covenant between God and every living creature on earth.*

Gen. 9:16 (NLT)

Spirituality is awe in the presence of every living thing; it lovingly respects all God's creatures and preserves them. They are as incomprehensible as we are, for we share the same Creator. It is not your power over other creatures that makes you human, but recognizing your responsibility for them. Don't feel superior to them; feel humbled by them. Take the time to look at any creature—a daisy, a spider. Really look at it, and you will humbly experience the intricacies of its existence and feel the significance of creation.

God's fingerprints are on every living being and thing in nature. The scriptures are printed on each leaf and every feather. Learn to read the sacred code: there are sermons in birds' chirpings; in the scent of blossoms, brush, stems, and petals; in the coolness of the wind and the warmth of the sun. There are hymns in the grass of cemeteries, canticles in the gently rustling breeze, and chants in waterfalls. All that is required is for you to immerse yourself in nature and be awed by it. In nature you do not need to seek, but you will be found. In communion with nature you are fully present and centered and a sense of clarity will come to you. If you sit and contemplate the vulnerability of a flower or of immense stellar distances, you'll find an intimation of divinity. It is the time for prayerfulness.

## OUR BODY IS A UNIVERSAL BODY

*We who are many form of one body*

Romans 12:5 (NIV)

God created a single body—nature. From this natural source each of us is given a share in the form of DNA, which is manifested in your present shape. In their essence all beings are homogeneous, though spectacularly heterogeneous in form. Each of us is like a hand-thrown clay pot holding a full measure of water that God has dipped from the immense ocean of life. Although each pot is shaped differently, the function is the same, and when the container pot breaks, the water eventually returns to the ocean.

The shapes, sizes, and colors of the containers holding the ocean water are so varied, we occasionally confuse their form with their essence. This confusion may result in your seeing race, sex, color as an "us and them" differentiation, which is the source of many of life's conflicts. This differentiation becomes even more acute when you see no connection between yourself and the rest of nature. You experience animals as enemies, vegetation as obstacles. In fact, humans, animals, and vegetation are related to each other and, more important, have the potential to sustain each other. It is only from such recognition that you can have a harmonious existence in the world.

## NATURE IS GOD'S ASSISTANT TEACHER

*The earth shall be full of the knowledge of the LORD*
*as the waters cover the sea.*

Isa. 11:9 (KJV)

An illiterate but holy man was asked what the source of his wisdom was. He replied that all he knew was in his Bible. When asked what exactly was in his Bible, he answered: "One pressed flower."

Although he couldn't read the words of God in the Bible, this man experienced one of His creations in depth. Every time the old man opened his Bible the pressed flower was there. He looked at it, really looked at it. In awe, he admired the subtleties of its colors and intricacies of its shape. He contemplated God in front of His creation and dissolved in them both. The wise man learned from nature by dissolving in it. So can you, by being not just part of nature, but by being it, as the rivers that lose themselves in the oceans. Don't settle by "being in it" or "being part of it" or "belonging to it." These emphasize the separateness from nature. As long as you maintain that distance you'll remain an observer. You'll be watching, admiring, liking, disliking, and fearing, but not dissolving in God.

We tend to attribute wisdom to the gurus of psychology and philosophy and to other learned men and women. No doubt, these people are well educated, smart, articulate. To us, they are extraordinary individuals; we try to comply with what they say and write. But meeting them in person is disappointing if their extraordinary intellectual depth is not matched by their emotional presence; that is, a corresponding spiritual depth. That is why the Bible says, *We . . . speak a message of wisdom among the mature, but not the wisdom of this age or of the rulers of this age.* (1 Cor. 2:6, NIV)

We are inclined to dismiss the wisdom of ordinary people, especially if they cannot articulate their experiences. When they do, we tend to give more weight to how these experiences are articulated than to the experiences themselves. You'll learn more by watching an ordinary gardener plant a bush than by attending a class in gardening. The wisdom of ordinariness is the accumulation of ordinary life experiences. If it is cultivated by holy living, this ordinary wisdom ultimately culminates in the extraordinary wisdom of spiritual maturity.

Carve out time to be alone in natural surroundings. How often do you look at the night sky and contemplate the stars and the mystery of the universe? Your life is probably so loaded with activities that you are never alone, never mind being alone in nature. No doubt social and professional obligations compound your already demanding family life so that you find sanctuary only in your sleep.

The solitude of nature replenishes. You occasionally need to reduce all stimuli—no matter how pleasant they may be—and experience (as much as possible) your own soundless internal harmony. You need to get in touch with your unfelt feelings and unthought thoughts and allow your mind slowly to become still. When external silence is joined with internal silence, chaotic thoughts and feelings transform into a harmonious and peaceful moment. There, you'll find a hint of eternal truth.

Nature teaches us about permanency in transience, stability in irregularity, and sameness in change. In nature, everything seems transient. Leaves fall off trees, trees fall, flowers dry up, the delightful breeze of summer ends, pets get old and die. And you may comment on how ephemeral everything is. But things in nature are ephemeral only if you look at them in an isolation-of-a-moment way. Leaves come back year after year, new shoots emerge from underneath fallen trees, and new puppies are born. Spring follows winter, fall follows summer. The temperature and precipitation may vary, but the sequence of seasons never changes. The sun, moon, stars are always in their regular places at any given hour, day, and month of the year. What else do you need to know to be convinced of the existence of eternity?

You can attain peace by learning from nature and connecting your transitory existence in this world to the permanence of eternity. This means ceasing to exist in any specific time and location. It means existing in all times and all locations and in all creatures of God.

# EXERCISES FOR PSYCHO-SPIRITUAL FITNESS

### THE WISDOM LEARNED FROM THE BIBLE

*God wants me to seek harmony in life.*

### MEDITATIVE EXERCISE OF SELF-REVELATION

*Have I been lovingly protective of God's creatures?*

### PRAYER EXERCISE OF GRATITUDE

*Dear God, thank You for Your creatures.*

### INTENTIONAL EXERCISE OF SPIRITUAL REALIGNMENT

*I'll commune with nature.*

## THINGS ARE VESSELS WITH WHICH WE SERVE GOD AS WE SERVE OURSELVES

*Yes, we should make the most of what God gives . . .*
*accepting what's given and delighting in the work.*
*It's God's gift!*

Eccles. 5:19 (MSG)

Soulful transformation is a type of alchemy. One part of it is within; the other part of it is in the outside world. The part within contains the emotions of love, caring, and attention. When these emotions encounter objects in the outside world (wood, metal, stone, paper), there occurs a soulful connection. When you make something new by combining your inner world's emotion and the outer world's resources—if you take pieces of raw wood and make a chair from them, for example—you will have served God.

You live among things; you possess and dispose of them. You adorn yourself with them, use them for protection and for transportation. You comb your hair, brush your teeth, and wash your body with them. You sit, sleep, and play on them.

- Take good care of things.
- Don't hoard.
- Empty the house.
- Wish for what you have.

Some things exist simply for us and would not exist independently of our need for them, such as cars, scissors, mirrors, chairs, beds, lamps, and curtains. We create these things for our own comfort, safety, and convenience. Treat these things as if they were precious, remembering that the Creator treats you as His precious creation. They will serve you better. A sharpened pencil helps you write more legibly, a dusted rug hosts fewer allergens, a polished table lasts longer, dried scissors don't rust, well-washed underwear won't irritate your skin, and a well-maintained car won't leave you stranded on the road.

Preoccupation with having possessions and acquiring more of them reflects a lack of depth. Rather, value what you have and take good care of those things. Having an appropriate attitude toward things generates a sensible philosophy of consumption. Accumulation of things undermines your sense of worth and generates a feeling of insatiability. Once you are trapped within insatiable desire, your spirit becomes stunted. Things can't fill the spiritual vacuum; if anything, they make the void larger. You can be fulfilled only when you are empty of the desire for more. Acquire fewer things and take good care of them. Every object that you have or make should be used as a vessel for serving God, even when it serves ourselves.

God creates every inanimate object, either through us or independent of us. You can see His fingerprints intertwined with your fingerprints. Therefore, you should treat inanimate objects with care and attention, if not awe and respect.

## WISH TO YEARN FOR NOTHING

*All things whatsoever you pray and ask for,*
*believe that you have received them.*

Mark 11:24 (NASB)

Peace does not come when you ask for something from God and then wait for its delivery. Peace comes when you thank God as if He has already answered your prayer. That is asking for what you have.

Value things, but do not become attached to them. The story of the monk and the rich man illustrates this point. A rich man visited with the custodian monk of a rundown shrine. Although the shrine had once been filled with life and faith, the sole occupant now was the monk. As a gesture of support for the holy place, the rich man handed the monk a large envelope filled with money. The monk took the money, handed the man a piece of paper and walked away. The paper was the deed to the shrine.

The shrine, without its monks, was an empty building, and as such it could be bought or sold. The monk's indifference to the building is the lesson of this tale. Peacefulness is cultivating holy indifference, a state of being unattached to things.

Too much of anything, including very good things, is bad for your soul. Drinking water and breathing air are essential for human life. But if you drink more water than your thirst dictates (on the average, eight to ten glasses a day), you can end up with water poisoning. Similarly, if you breathe more air than your lungs demand (about 20 to 25 respirations per minute at rest), you'll faint. If you try to hoard air or water, you'll hurt yourself. Moses advised the Jews on the Exodus from Egypt to eat as much manna (a kind of coriander seed) as would fill them, but not to carry more than they could eat because the manna spoiled within a day and would be a fertile breeding ground for worms.

Instead of owning dozens of pairs of shoes, if you have just a few, you'll get to know them. They'll have a life with you. Your shoes will get you to work, take you to visit friends, bring you back home. A well-worn shoe conveys a sense of familiarity. People who have many shoes may not even remember whether or not they have a certain pair or when they bought them, or even whether they wear comfortably or not; they are strangers. If you wear such shoes, you'll be aware of your feet and feel a little unsteady, if not insecure, in your steps.

Some people have more than they need but they still buy, and if they cannot buy things, they wish they could. For such people life becomes a preoccupation with possessions. Buying more does not satisfy the wish to own; it leaves the person yearning. These people are chronically unsatisfied and frustrated. No object satisfies that yearning. Not only are these people ungrateful for what they already have, they are also envious of others, even of those who are less fortunate. If they succeed in life, they are constantly anxious. If they fail, they are engulfed in a rage-filled depression. Only spiritual satiety—wishing for what you have—lightens your soul.

## WE ARE ALL PASSING THROUGH

*So we fix our eyes not on what is seen, but on what is unseen.*
*For what is seen is temporary, but what is unseen is eternal.*

2 Cor. 4:18 (NIV)

There is a story of a wise man who was visited by many people each day. One visitor was shocked to see that the wise man's house was nearly empty except for two wooden chairs, a table, and a narrow bed. "Where is your furniture?" the visitor asked. "Where is yours?" asked the old man. "I am only passing through," the tourist replied. "So am I," said the old man.

We are all passing through. When we die, all our precious things escape our tightest grasp; suddenly they belong to someone else—for the time being. The house you carefully designed and built; the business you so determinedly negotiated; the sweaters you lovingly protected from moths; ties, dresses, suits you saved for specific occasions and never wore; jewelry and watches you worried might be stolen—all of these things will someday suddenly no longer belong to you.

If you understand that there is no connection between possession and immortality, you will be burdened only with what you need and nothing more. If you also understand that you are simply a caretaker of things during your lifetime, guaranteeing the safe transfer of these things to the next generation, you will take good care of your temporary possessions. God has loaned you whatever you are enjoying right now with the expectation that you'll pass it on in as good (if not in better) shape to the next person. I knew a man who fixed up and painted his house *after* he sold it. He told me he wanted to deliver this "gift" from God to the next owner.

When you receive anything—a house, jewelry—from a stranger, even though you paid for it, it is, in fact, a gift from God. Treat these things with loving care before you pass them on to another stranger. We are only vehicles of God for the safe passage of His creations.

# EXERCISES FOR PSYCHO-SPIRITUAL FITNESS

### THE WISDOM LEARNED FROM THE BIBLE

*God wants me to be filled only with the Spirit.*

### MEDITATIVE EXERCISE OF SELF-REVELATION

*Have I emptied my mind of preoccupation with worldly possessions?*

### PRAYER EXERCISE OF GRATITUDE

*Dear God, thank You for helping me learn from austerity.*

### INTENTIONAL EXERCISE OF SPIRITUAL REALIGNMENT

*I'll be joyful with what I have.*

## DON'T BE AFRAID OF DYING

*Come before him, singing with joy.*

Ps. 100:2 (NLT)

This world is to live in and to die in as well. Few of us are afraid of living but most of us are afraid of dying. Death seems to be a most formidable enemy. Death is not the enemy; fear of it is. The certainty of death is your birthright and a source of rebirth. With death you'll finally go home: darkness is just a passage to the ultimate light, and physical losses are a prelude to spiritual union. When the Bible says, *The last enemy to be destroyed is death,* (1 Cor. 15:26, NIV) it speaks of destroying the fear of death, fear of the unknown, fear of the end, and fear of disappearing.

The inevitability of dying was placed in our minds when God *planted eternity in the human heart.* (Eccles. 3:11, NLT) Perfect harmony comes when your mind is subordinate to your heart; that is, when trust dissipates fear. The more you trust in God, the less you will be afraid of dying. The Bible says, *The Lord gives perfect peace to those whose faith is firm.* (Isa. 26:3, CEV)

- Live life but don't hold it tightly.
- Seek the inner light hidden in darkness.
- Live your death.
- Joyfully anticipate your incorporeal continuum.

You die a little death every night and are born every morning. In between, you lose your grasp on everything you have. Whether one day you can gently go to your death depends on how covetous you are of life. "I'll die because I am alive," said a faithful man who had lived every moment of his life. A spiritual man knew he was going home by way of his terminal cancer and he left while fully living his death. He quoted the Bible: *"I want to finish the race I am running."* (Acts 20:24, GWT) To a woman who lost her infant to crib death, nothing was of consolation until the day she really heard that her loss wasn't a loss for God. "I gave the child back," she said. We all need to taste death and, like these faithful individuals, to understand death.

The fear of death comes from living in the howling darkness of aloneness—without God to worship and without a worshipping family, friends, and community. People whose souls are deprived of spiritual illumination neither live a good life nor die a holy death. In fact, they die in life. For them, life is a journey to meaningless oblivion. But if you are a spiritual light-bearer or just imbued with even one beam of divine light, you'll know how to make both life and death meaningful. You'll live life in such a way that you'll never be afraid to die. The fear of the end of the journey preempts the journey itself. The importance of the journey is in experiencing its moments and living thoroughly to its end.

When the time comes, you need not do anything but sail into the mystery of God in His ship. As the passenger of a ship advances only by the movement of the ship, so too will you advance without any movement on your part.

## ON OUR DEATHBED THE ONLY THING WE WANT TO KNOW IS THAT WE WERE LOVED

*I want your constant love.*

Hos. 6:6 (GNT)

You may have witnessed people with terminal illnesses or those who are close to death. Their eyes plead for help in easing their painful loneliness. They seek reassuring love and hope. They lose all their interest in worldly matters such as bank accounts, cars, houses, titles, clothes, and jewelry. Most people on their deathbeds would like to be forgiven for past transgressions against their loved ones, no matter how insignificant the damage might have been. That request for forgiveness is not geared primarily toward soothing guilt but toward reaffirming love. At that time, the cusp of life becomes a blade severing the ties to living and our final message is uttered in silence: "I loved you. Tell me that you loved me."

## ONLY SPIRITUAL DEATH IS REALLY FRIGHTENING

*Those who know Your name will put their trust in You.*
*For You, O Lord, have never left alone those who look for You.*

Ps. 9:10 (NLV)

"Dust to dust" is not metaphorical. At the end, all that is left of you is the dust that makes up the earth. *All life comes from the ground and all of it goes back to the ground.* (Eccles. 3:20, GWT) But that is only your body.

When you die, your body is put in a grave, but not your soul. *The wind blows wherever it pleases. You hear its sound, but you don't know where the wind comes from or where it's going. That's the way it is with everyone born of the Spirit.* (John 3:8, GWT) The souls of the spiritual are never entombed with their bodies. But if you live a totally nonspiritual life, your body will become the tomb of your soul.

Being peaceful means having sacred optimism and expectations about everything, whether it is about the birth of a child, your life, the passing of a parent, or your own impending death. Sacred optimism is the realization of knowing that the sun is shining behind the clouds. Such a positive outlook, in return, brings about the best outcomes. Optimism is faithfulness. The prism of faith catches the light and disperses it on every aspect of your life, whether it is health, work satisfaction, marital contentment, or death. Pessimism is spiritual starvation. Seeing the world through the no-faith prism is simply a misunderstanding of life. Pessimism is misinterpretation of reality, like emphasizing that the sun is always setting somewhere. Viewing death in a negative way is such a misinterpretation.

Make optimism a ritual in your daily life and you will die a spiritual death. These daily rituals need not be religious to be spiritual. They can be rituals that convey love (like a woman who phoned her friends every Sunday just to say hello and inquire about their lives); gratitude (like a man who added "thank you" notes anytime he paid his bills); respect (like a person who called her housekeeper by her last name, using *Mrs.*); kindness (like a husband who offered only compliments when his wife got dressed to go out); humility (like a person who never interrupted people in the middle of their conversations, no matter how long-winded they were); and cheerfulness (like the parents who woke their children with big smiles and "good mornings" and put them to bed with stories conveying faithful optimism and happy tidings). You need to cultivate your own positive rituals and integrate them as spiritual energy savers into your daily life. A friend made "positive priming" his ritual. Whenever he is about to say "I won't," he says, "I will." Instead of "I won't be impatient," he says, "I will be patient." As to dying, instead of saying, "I won't be afraid of death" say, "I'll welcome death when the time comes."

The Bible asks us, *What is life?* then tells us, *You are a mist that is seen for a moment and then disappears.* (James 4:14, GWT) Spiritual peacefulness comes from recognizing that we are transient in our present forms, but eternal in "no form." The Bible says, *Our days on earth are like a shadow.* (1 Chron. 29:15, NIV) The dread of no longer being—the eternal absence—is related to our misunderstanding of time. "Eternity" doesn't mean endless time; it means no time.

We know from science that our body is representative of the world body; that is, it is made of organic and inorganic substances, as are all other creatures. Structures formed by these substances have limited lives. When all the cells of our body return to their original state, they'll be poised to serve in the formation of a new creature. While anything alive is on a celestial pilgrimage of dying, it simultaneously secures the inexhaustible source of life. The Bible says, *Anyone who holds on to life just as it is, destroys that life.* (John 12:25, MSG)

Our souls are timeless and formless. The Bible says, *As there is a physical body, so there is also a spiritual body.* (1 Cor. 15:44, GWT) The rhythm of the sun and the moon is your witness to timelessness; their beams are formless. Travel in them until you are them. Your soul is not to be equated with cells of your body. The soul exists in one host form or another, but it has no form itself. This formlessness is what makes the soul eternal. It never exists nor does it cease to exist in the usual sense of understanding existence.

Eternal life is life in God's essence. You need not anguish about the future, nor long for it; rather, just drink deeply from the Holy Well with tender trust. Faith lowers the heavens to earth and raises cemeteries to the heavens.

# EXERCISES FOR PSYCHO-SPIRITUAL FITNESS

**THE WISDOM LEARNED FROM THE BIBLE**

*God wants you to come home in exultation.*

**MEDITATIVE EXERCISE
OF SELF-REVELATION**

*Have I been putting my trust in God?*

**PRAYER EXERCISE OF GRATITUDE**

*Dear God, thank You for planting eternity
in my heart.*

**INTENTIONAL EXERCISE
OF SPIRITUAL REALIGNMENT**

*I'll hold on loosely to my life.*

*The Bible, it began with man's search for God, and ended with God finding man.*

Anonymous, 2005

# I BELIEVE IN GOD, THEREFORE I AM

> *Now all has been heard; here is the*
> *conclusion of the matter:*
>
> *Fear God and keep His command-*
> *ments,*
>
> *For this is the whole duty of man.*
>
> Eccles. 12:13 (NIV)

## THE BIBLE IS THE ONLY SELF-HELP BOOK YOU NEED

In the academic world, there are philosophers who try to make sense of human beings by defining us through our abilities to think and feel. They even use maxims, such as "I think" or "I feel . . . therefore I am," to assert that feeling and thinking differentiate us humans from other beings. They emphasize that through our feelings, for example, we all learn to love or hate, experience pain and pleasure, be happy or depressed. Through our thinking, we understand, explain, justify, or even rationalize our sentiments and behavior as we try to make sense of the world.

Equally, in our private worlds, we all try to make sense of

ourselves by developing personal philosophies of life. These philosophies tend to stem from our attempts to cope with misfortune in life. For example, you may believe that there are no permanent friends, only permanent interests, or that marriage is an artificial institution, or that parenthood and creativity are mutually exclusive, or that success sometimes requires crossing ethical boundaries. Such pessimistic views of life simply generate cynicism, despair, and hopelessness.

Conversely, secular optimistic views about life are useful but they are time- and situation-limited. You may believe that to love is to learn or that a circle of friends is your alternative family, or that marriage and parenthood are a responsibility, or that one sows what one reaps, or that illnesses and losses are part of life. As true as these statements are, they'll not survive life's adversities unless they become grounded in the permanency of God's view. The Bible says, *The grass withers and the flowers fall, but the word of . . . God stands forever.* (Isa. 40:8, NIV)

There are also popular self-help books promoting various philosophies of "self-centering" and "now." The full development of self, however, cannot be cultivated in a self-centered life, nor can a full awareness of the present take place without resonance with the past and the future. Literal "self-centering" and "now" orientations condemn a person to live in the isolation of the self and in the exile of the present. The only "now" worth cultivating is the "eternal now," and the only "self-centering" worth preserving is "eternal centering." Living a full life while serving your own interest is best accomplished by decentering yourself now and remaining God-centered eternally.

The only philosophy you need is, "I believe in God; therefore I am." God helps you understand and explain yourself and your relationships, as well as helping you understand the world. You'll not need sundry self-help books on how to succeed, how to have a happy marriage, how to raise children, or how to be wise or spiritual. The only self-help book you need is the Bible. The Bible is the ultimate self-help book, as well as the ultimate book on psychology and philosophy.

## PRACTICE FOR SPIRITUAL LITERACY

*Now that you know these things,*
*you will be blessed if you do them.*

John 13:17 (NIV)

Once upon a time there was an impoverished small town in which there were only four old clocks. One day all of them stopped working, and there was no clockmaker to fix them. So they were all left to rust, except one, which was oiled and cleaned and wound by the town fool as the cynical villagers looked on. One day, a watchmaker came to town and found all the clocks beyond repair but one—the town fool's clock.

Equally, your spirituality needs tending even if it seems broken and beyond repair. The tending of the spirit is a joyous act, but it requires patience and diligence and staying power, especially in the absence of immediate, visible, audible, or tangible results.

As a practitioner of spirituality, you may find yourself criticized and even treated as a fool by your own "villagers."

Don't be dissuaded, shamed, or discouraged. Keep reading and rereading the Bible and meditating on it. One day you'll be visited and you'll be exalted. The Bible says, *Do not let this Book of the Law depart from your mouth; meditate on it day and night. . . . Then you will be prosperous and successful.* (Josh. 1:8, NIV)

# KEY TO BIBLICAL ABBREVIATIONS

I have quoted different translations of the Bible to find the best phrases in order to highlight specific points in the simplest terms and expressions closest to the contemporary language. The quotations are used by permission.

AMP             The Amplified Bible. © 1954, 1958, 1962, 1964, 1965, 1987, by The Lockman Foundation. Grand Rapids, MI: Zondervan Publishing.

ASV             American Standard Version. © 1901. Public Domain.

CEV             Contemporary English Version. © 1995. New York: American Bible Society.

ESV             The Holy Bible, English Standard Version. © 2001. Wheaton, IL: Crossway Bibles, a division of Good News Publishers.

GNT             Good News Translation, Second Edition. © 1992. New York: American Bible Society.

GWT             GOD'S WORD®. © 1995. Orange Park, FL: God's Word to the Nations.

KJV
King James Version. 1987. Public Domain in the United States. Accessed at www.biblegateway.com.

MSG
*The Message.* © 1993, 1994, 1995, 1996, 2000, 2001, 2002. Colorado Springs, CO: NavPress Publishing.

NASB
New American Standard Bible. © 1960, 1962, 1963, 1968, 1971, 1972, 1973, 1975, 1977, 1995. La Habra, CA: The Lockman Foundation.

NCV
New Century Version. © 1987, 1988, 1991. Nashville, TN: World Publishing, a division of Thomas Nelson, Inc.

NIV
Holy Bible, New International Version®. © 1973, 1978, 1984. Colorado Springs, CO: International Bible Society.

NIV-UK
Holy Bible, New International Version®. © 1973, 1978, 1984. Colorado Springs, CO: International Bible Society.

NKJV
New King James Version. © 1982. Nashville, TN: Thomas Nelson, Inc.

NLT
Holy Bible. New Living Translation. © 1996. Carol Stream, IL: Tyndale House Publishers.

NLV
The New Life Version. © 1969. Canby, OR: Christian Literature International.

NWT
New World Translation of the Holy Scriptures. 1961. Brooklyn, NY: Watchtower Bible and Tract Society of New York.

Ph          J. B. Phillips, trans. The New Testament in Modern
            English. © 1996. New York: Touchstone.

RSV         The New Oxford Annotated Bible, with the Apoc-
            rypha. Revised standard version, edited by Herbert
            Gordon May and Bruce Manning Metzger. © 1977.
            New York: Oxford University Press.

WE–NT       Worldwide English–New Testament. © 1996. Will-
            ington, Derby, UK: SOON Educational Publica-
            tions.

# CITATIONS FOR CHAPTER-OPENING QUOTATIONS

## Chapter I

*There is naught in the Gospels, which does not shine*
*and illuminate the world by its splendor, so that even*
*things that seem trifling and unimportant shine with*
*the majesty of the Holy Spirit.*

St. Jerome. This reference is originally from the writings of Saint Jerome's Commentary on Ezekiel (1:4–28) and, in particular, Ezekiel (1:15–18). Saint Jerome's writings are not directly available. This reference is quoted in Pope Benedict XV's Encyclicals: Spiritus Paraclitus on St. Jerome to all the Patriarchs, Primates, Archbishops, Bishops, and Ordinaries in Union with the Apostolic See (given at Saint Peter's, September 15, 1920; paragraph #13).

## Chapter II

*I wish to show that there is one wisdom which is per-*
*fect, and that this is contained in the Scriptures.*

Roger Bacon. *The Opus Majus of Roger Bacon.* Translated by Robert Belle Burke. New York: Russell and Russell, Inc., vol. I (Part II, Chapter I), 1962, p. 36.

## Chapter III

> *For I am not qualified to have dreams or to explain them, nor do I seek this ability or knowledge for myself, and I have concluded a pact with my Lord God that He should not send me visions or dreams or even angels. For I am content with this gift which I have, Holy Scripture, which abundantly teaches and supplies all things necessary for both this life and also for the life to come.*

Martin Luther. Luther's works. Vol. 6: Lectures on Genesis. St. Louis, MO: Concordia, 1970.

## Chapter IV

> *Scripture is the school of the Holy Spirit, in which, as nothing is omitted that is both necessary and useful to know, so nothing is taught but what is expedient to know.*

John Calvin. *Institutes of the Christian Religion.* Christian Classics Ethereal Library. Accessed January 24, 2005. Available from http://www.ccel.org/ccel/calvin/institutes.htm.

## Chapter V

> *A little philosophy inclineth man's mind to atheism, but depth in philosophy bringeth men's minds about to religion.*

Francis Bacon. The Essays. 1601. The University of Adelaide. Accessed January 25, 2005, and May 2, 2005. Available from

http://etext.library.adelaide.edu.au/b/bacon/francis/b12e/part15
.html.

## Chapter VI

*When the Doctrine of the Gospel becomes the Reason
of our Mind, it will become the Principle of our Life.*

Benjamin Whichcote, D.D., *Morals and Religious Aphorisms*, with
an introduction by William Ralph Inge, D.D. London: Elkin
Mathews & Marrot, Ltd., 1930, p. 12 (aphorism #94).

## Chapter VII

*What are all the gifts of the Gospel; are they not all
mental gifts . . . And are not the gifts of the Spirit everything to man?*

G. Keynes, ed. *The complete writings of William Blake: With all
the variant readings.* Nonesuch Press, 1957. Available from
www.Questia.com.

## Chapter VII

*[The Bible] is the best book that ever was or ever will
be known in the world . . . because it teaches you the
best lessons by which any human creature who tries to
be truthful and faithful to duty can possibly be guided.*

Charles Dickens. *The letters of Charles Dickens, edited by his sister-
in-law and his eldest daughter.* Chapman and Hall, 1880. Accessed
January 21, 2005. Available from http://victorian.lang.nagoya
u.ac.jp/concordance/dickens.

## Chapter IX

*Any group of men, however ignorant, need only to be able to read the Bible to be in possession of the ultimate, undeniable truth about almost any important question of human life.*

Everett Dean Martin, *Liberty*. W.W. Norton, 1930. Accessed April 29, 2005. Available from www.Questia.com.